And Then I Woke Up: Poems, Writings, Confessions, and Ramblings

Printed in the United States of America

First Printing: March 2011

ISBN: 9781613641675

And Then I Woke Up:
Poems, Thoughts, Confessions, and Ramblings

By: Charles L. Crouch

This book is dedicated to the brother in IHOP:

Around 1995 I was standing in line at IHOP with some of my homies, trying to portray something I wasn't.

I noticed you staring at me. It was a stare so intense that I felt uncomfortable and defensive at the same time.

You walked up to me with no fear, and told me the Hand of God was on my life.

No fanfare, no title, no name, no "God told me to tell you", just brother to brother realness.

I never forgot that brother. I don't know if you were an angel or not, but thank you sir.

You changed my life that day.

TABLE OF CONTENTS

Introduction

If you were to look in the bottom drawer of my filing cabinet you would see a particularly flimsy, old, rugged folder. This folder is complete with Kool-Aid stains, rips, tears, various notes, phone numbers, reminders in pen, and a faint label that says, "Misc. Poems, and Writings." If you were to dig a little deeper you would see many notebooks, tablets, loose leaf paper, and poetic diaries full of writings dating back to 1999. Through several moves to different apartments, and houses over the years, this particular folder is probably the most important thing that is held sacred. It does not get thrown in with the rest of the stuff. When the U-Haul is all packed up with couches, beds, and dressers, best believe that this folder is in the front seat. It has been the subject of many arguments...many debates...many tears. This folder holds my life story...my feelings...my rage...my loves...my fears...my secrets...my soul.

One obscure thing about many poets is that we do not talk much. Rarely will we inject our opinions, verbally, unless we are asked to, and even think we still may decline.

Many of us feel like others will not understand us. We are quiet, introverted people. To put it simply; we write our feelings down more than vocally expressing them. It dawned on me about a year ago exactly how much written emotion I had acquired over the years. It is literally hundreds of pieces; to the point where it is almost autobiographical. This is not counting the many impromptu pieces that were written on scraps of paper in doctor's office waiting rooms, and lunch breaks that ended up in my pocket only to be mistakenly washed in the washing machine. These were probably some of the most heartfelt pieces I had written.

When I first began writing poetry seriously I was literally writing something every single day. Many thoughts I had including: social issues, relationship woes, love, spiritual dilemmas, apprehensions about people, religion, and fears were written about. At one point there were, literally, poems everywhere in my room. There were so many poems; in fact, I would forget where I put them; many of which were left unfinished. Many were thrown away due to frustration levels when writing. A few poems were found by people who were not suppose to see them; causing me to have to explain what I meant in the expression. From that point on, I learned to write in a poetic code. It is a code called "abstract writing" in the artistic world. Much like abstract art, poetic abstractness sometimes may only be understood by the writer; leaving the readers free to formulate their own theories as to hidden meanings.

The more and more I let people read my work, the more I realized that many people shared my sentiments; they just did not know how to express them. It also let me know that I was not the only person who felt a certain way about certain things, and the hidden opinion I deemed unpopular was not that unpopular after all. I was not the only person that dealt with certain demons. It let me know that I had a gift that could touch other people.

In my last book I mentioned King David as being one of my favorite Biblical figures. Great deals of King David's thoughts were chronicled. We call them Psalms. The Book of Psalms, along with Job, Ecclesiastes, Proverbs, and The Song Of Solomon, is one of the Biblical books of poetry. I will venture to say that Psalms is the most popular, and probably the most quoted. David's victories, his fears, his strengths, his weaknesses, his indiscretions, his adoration for God, his worship, his praise, his soft spot for beautiful women, his lookout on society, his spiritual dilemmas; everything was documented. David was a very open man.

With that being said, I consider this to be my personal collection of Psalms in a sense. Now don't get your feathers all ruffled due to that statement. I am not comparing myself to King David in the least bit. The reason I am calling this my collection of Psalms is mainly because, like the Psalms in the Bible, there is no particular order in which these writings flow. You will see certain patterns in my writing. Some will be very self explanatory, while others may be a bit confusing; hence a word in the subtitle: Ramblings. This is a somewhat autobiographical, poetic representation of my life. Make no mistake; many of these poems are raw and honest. There is subject matter in some of these that are definitely for adults. I am not one to use profanity in my poetry; however, some things mentioned pierce the soul deeper than any vulgar word can.

Perhaps you will see yourself in some of these poems. Then again, you may not. There may be poems that bring out issues that may have been buried in your past. That's the beautiful thing about poetry; it makes you deal with issues that may be a hindrance to progression. Many of these pieces have the same theme. However, there are worded differently to express my feelings towards a subject matter at that particular time.

I decided to release these writings so that people will understand the mind of a black man. These are poems written from the perspective of a black man who has lived a full, yet sometimes mentally and emotionally sheltered life. Many people only know me as the guy who read a few poems in church on special holidays such as Mother's Day, and Father's Day. Others know me as the love hungry brother who adores his black woman. Then there are some who know me as the soft spoken dude who releases his emotion towards the trials, struggles, triumphs, and ailments of his people through his poetry, lectures, motivational speeches, and music. There are some women who know me as the man who broke their heart; one who was, at times, too honest or too secretive. Some call me friend, some call me brother, some call me son, some call me mentor, some call me a teacher, some call me confused, and there are some that will never call me again. So I will let you decide. These poems are my thoughts, my confessions, and my ramblings. The revelation always seems to come after you wake up. Thus, "Then I Woke Up"...and these were my thoughts, my words, and my soul.

Poems and Thoughts

Cracked Thoughts

You ever wonder what a crackhead thinks about right before he hits the pipe? I don't know...probably a whole lot of mistakes in life. Ever wonder what he thinks about when he first lights it up? He's probably hoping the issues will disappear and it would be his last time here...in this position. Wishing he never took that first initial pull...full of hurt and anger...as he knows the danger of losing his family; but in his earthly strength...he can't kick the habit. Hopefully the high will make life better and he won't have to keep reliving his faults, mistakes and bad breaks and he hopes that when he wakes up in the morning...he beholds a new creature. But it never happens. It never changes. "Rearrange my life," he thinks...but the pipe is his best friend. Yet nobody has the power to hurt you like your friends. Nobody has the power to cheer you up like your friends. Nobody can tell you about yourself quite like your friends. Then I wonder if he sees himself in the glass reflection of the pipe. Does he see himself or his wealth going down the drain? Does he see the pain of his childhood? Misunderstood? Missed good opportunities? A unity gone sour? Hour after hour the cocaine rapes his brain and his soul it devours. He cleans himself up to face the rest of the world...but...

Showers never clean up the inside of a man.

Showers never clean up the inside of a man.

He takes a pull. Instantly he has visions of prosperous children and a loving wife...chemically charged mental portraits of a life of financial security blocks out the reality that he has a $500 per day habit. Thus he grabs it and hits it again then he thinks..."This pipe is my friend."

"My best friend"..."My worst enemy"..."My best enemy"..."My worst friend"...means the same. Contradiction. Once contra-addiction, now going into reverse remission...again.

Relapse.

Perhaps those who make love to the hard white are quite like us.

Are we are all crackheads...with crack coming in various forms?

See for me...my crack is poems.

Your crack may be the bottle...prescriptions or alcohol, music or domestic abuse. We are trying to call a truce between our mistakes and your guilty conscience with the contents of earthly sedatives...but we let it live...and live...without ever spiritually dealing with the problem.

So let me ask.

What is your crack?

Insomnia

How long does it take for this sleeping pill to infiltrate my bloodstream?

I need to dream.

I need to dream.

I need to scheme up ways to save the world...save the boys and girls and hurl knowledge pieces to the masses for the *mass is* dying slowly.

I need yesterday to resurrect so I can mold a better "now" for my seeds because the future looks dim for them.

It looks grim as the rim of my communion glass is overflowing; over knowing that Christ is crucified daily because of our ignorance.

My people are perishing for a lack of knowledge and wisdom...gives them the right to do wrong...left to sing these slave songs glorifying bling-bling and King's dream seems nightmarish. Why perish when our forefathers have already died...for the cause?

At times I think slow so I can fast for understanding.

At times I think fast so I can be slow to speak.

At times I speak fast because I wonder if those very words will be my last.

I'd die for my righteous cause.

Cash rules everything around but everything around me, it seems, is poverty-stricken...As my mind's clock keeps ticking.

I write to the depths of my mind's tears.

So many blind years...as many define their fears in blank dictionaries because they have none. Not even fear for the Righteous Son.

Reality is blinded by superficiality as the fallacies and immorality tells us that living for self is wealth.

We are living in the neo dark ages...as my seed inwardly rages...telling me that it is much brighter in the womb.

How long will we consume our seed's time for crime and money, G-note stack dreams and cream?

And I feel it entering my bloodstream now.

I am getting sleepy now.

My eyelids like paperweights now...as I crawl into fetal position hoping to be reborn in the morn.

I want to rest peacefully like my unborn that is resting in the bosom of Christ.

I am wishing to make love, somehow, to wisdom and understanding; hoping that I can conceive future Martins', and Marcus', far from this crazed world full of platinum

gods who encourage our kids to stay fly and get high...and
more higher...calling ignorance "sire".

We chant these ghetto anthems as if we were never an
innovative people.

Our knowledge has become residual.

Ignorance has become mainstream, as the main theme in
my son's music is money, power, and murder.

I am barely awake.

Rarely do I take time to pray for self...but I feel as if my
prayers for my people are exhausted...as I am.

I consistently pray for "fam" but right now *I am*...in need of
strength.

I Am Blackness

I am that Negro Spiritual...I am the crack addicted child
that was a miracle.

I am the meaning of hope...I am the rehabilitated father
that used to snort coke...

I am the clip in Malcolm's rifle.

The overtime worked for a family's survival. I am the picket
sign from bus boycotts.

I am the peace rally that didn't bust shots...

I am the passion in a Donny Hathaway hook.

The enlightenment in a Black History book...

I am the sound of the gavel that freed Mandela...

I am the jazz riff in song that was sang by Ella.

I am love. I am peace. I am violence when my cries for
equality were silenced.

I am the welfare check for single mothers.

When the heat is cut off; I am the extra covers...

I am the gun that jammed before a black's man homicide...

The liquor poured out when young brother dies.

I am the tears from his mother...

I am the Rest in Peace tattoo that's inked on his brother.

I am the gang bandana that was burned...

I am the corporate America respect that was hard to earn.

I am Jesse Owens's gold medal...

I am the racial profiling case that was never settled.

I am the map for the Underground Railroad...

I am the inspiration in James Brown's soul...

I am the swing in Bob Marley's locks...

I am the unsolved murders of BIG and Tupac.

I am the chord structure of Thelonius...

I am the overlooked brother when jobs pass out bonuses.

I am Joe Clark's bat...

I am the stripes on a runaway slaves bloody back.

I am Angela Davis' Afro pick...

I am Magic's no look pass. I am Pele's kick.

I am hurt. I am struggle. I am pain. I am the levee that collapsed during Katrina's rain...

I am the Black Panther's anger.

I am the prayer that black men won't become a species that's endangered...

I am the bus pass for the brother's who's struggling.

I am the 9 to 5 for my man who's tired of hustling...

I am the wisdom in barbershop ciphers.

I am the Quran found by 25 to lifers...

I am of Simon of Cyrene when Jesus was weak...

I am the passion when a brother rubs his girl's feet.

I am the microphone when King said I Have A Dream...

I am the hope that Obama does the same thing.

I am the spear of Shaka Zulu...

I am the leadership of Desmond Tutu.

The innocence of Mumia...

I am the beautiful memory of Aaliyah.

I am the question that Marvin couldn't answer...

I am the music played when Luther and his father were dancers.

I am blackness...

I am music...I am sports...I am knowledge...I am peace, the struggle, the strength, the slavery abolished.

A Time for Fatherhood

There is nothing that can convince me that the authority in your voice could not cause the Himalayas to tremble a little...not to belittle the structure of nature, but your voice made ya stop and listen.

Something about the strength in your character that can evoke a household's dilemma into peace.

The way you strategically, yet seemingly easily, carry burdens and marry the hurting of others and divorce your issues to hand tissues from your soul to hold someone else together...amazes me.

You stand for righteousness at all costs...carry the cross for the family while travelling towards what seems to be a modern day Calvary from a distance...when it's existence is actually a peaceful promised land.

Rough hands...

Your body carries the scars, pain and the lineage of our forefather's years of whipped backs and attacks with water hoses and Civil Rights marches, yet you spark this light inside of you that still shines throughout the years...throughout the tears...throughout the fears...that you never let show.

You are the epitome of strength.

A pillar of knowledge and wisdom...Skilled craftsman of all trades...Disciplinarian, it was scary when I knew my mischief would warrant the lashes of belt to my backside...but it made me think twice about life's decisions. See you work overtime to make sure Christmas time over into more debt. You set the standard for the brother I am this day. So now I walk this way like Run DMC because I *really understand, now, dad's moral convictions.*

You are my father. The man who held me through storms and would warn me of danger as a young man, but let of my hand so I could learn from mistakes because I never knew how hot the oven was until I touched it...even after we discussed it. Sometimes learning the hard way makes you wise...I look in your eyes and I see my own personal Dr. King, Dr. Huxtable, Superman, mechanic, therapist, pharmacist, family doctor, lawyer, pathway to Heaven, James Evans when times got rough...you stood tough as a father should...and held the family together.

You taught me to plan instead of react, so I wouldn't re-enact the trap that turned my father's father's father into a martyr.

Thick skin and broad shoulders, God told us to honor your authority, assured me that the only minority is those that think they are better than the other man. Brother man with the plan to stand, other than God I don't think I show more reverence to any man.

And I know I am blessed because many young brothers today don't have father's who display character, they are caricatures of stereotypical, mystical creatures who their son can only dream about because they only hear about them gangster tales, and crack sells, hug them through jail cells, mailed child support checks, whose mother was merely a booty call, and when duty calls for the responsibility of fatherhood to be resumed, young men are left feeling like worthless trash because pops decided to litter inside of mother's womb. But you groomed me into the man I am today...and I thank you pop...

There is no one quite like you.

I love you...Your son.

Poem of the Spirit

I run speedily to knowledge feasts...as I dine at wisdom's dinner table. I am eternally fasting from ignorance as butterfly wings spread in my mind while I refrain from cocooned thoughts of closed mindedness. The bright lights of spiritual enlightenment blind me best as my mind's eye maintains 20/20 vision. More than twenty to infinity missions I embark upon as my mind continues to war.

Using any theorem, my sons multiplied by me equals destiny's children to infinite degrees...as sin flies right to me but I duck and dodge iniquity's attacks for the sake of my son.

Christ times me times poetry times my seeds feeds my soul equations to the 7th degree equaling a completed generational piece. I release quests from my soul that my offspring can travel my un-treaded spiritual Miles...Davis blows trumpets lines reminiscent of Gabriel calling prosperity through music and renaissance.

Inwardly I am warring silently, violently and quietly I rage wars on my past sins that I may proceed to reign in these present day battles.

Incessant babble runs free in my mind sometimes making the audience in my soul's open mic sessions "boo" me repeatedly off stage...because, at times, my words don't link. I think twice before speaking so my penny thoughts can be at least worth two cents...yet I must proceed in spite of my mind's warped illusions.

Delusions make my rainy days sometimes appear to be those of cherry picking mornings...warning myself that I must remain alert.

Overt biblical passages stick to my spirit and soul and whole thoughts of my destiny are inseparable.

Reputable...my sons shall be named.

Virtuous...my daughters shall stand and every man, child and woman of my spiritual tribe will lord over villages in the next millennium.

I don't go against the grain, the grain goes against me...thus I run free and not ashamed in unmarked land because I was cast out of common society.

I am a peculiar species. See these gentiles don't understand my spiritual thought pattern as I scatter poetic/Biblical knowledge pieces to the predators who crave the blood of my pen.

I comprehend the incomprehensible through the principles taught by the Lamb slain.

I live my life in Ecclesiastical theatricals because I got Christ on the brain.

I missed the train...thus I walk on muddy waters, sort of like Peter, and don't need an umbrella because I fear not the rain.

On Calvary, Christ bore my pain. My name is written in the Lamb's book.

I swim in brooks of wisdom and direction as my affections are set on things

above. Dove wings cover me...Color me white because I have been remitted of my sins. Wins...I have many. I refuse to lose. I refuse to choose the wide-open road because I walk the straight and narrow. I would rather dwell in the trees than with these modern day Pharisees because at least I know His eye is on the sparrow.

My soul...My life...My thoughts...My will...My mind...My time...My pennies...My dimes all belong to the Most High Jehovah who reigns and this is my poem of the spirit.

In Equality

What lies *in equality*? *Inequality* can't lie *in equality* because they mean the opposite, so composite sketches of me can't be etched into your mind because that would be stereotyping...wiping me off as the last because I am usually first in the lineup of suspects. Drug checks ran on me by the protectors and the servers of the community causes bitterness on my part because in my heart...I know that I am no criminal. Minimal minds that can't see beyond my skin tone roam speedily past me because they feel as if I am a threat but yet...we scream "we are all equal." *Inequality*, I see often because *any quality* I have that is of the positive is overlooked, as I am overbooked in my mind because so many of kind are hated against, discriminated against pushed to the fence to be searched...when only doing 8 miles over the speed limit. I am timid even when I am driving, as some conniving officers often mentally serve me warrants even before I am approached. I am reproached, re-choked by the nooses that used to hang my forefathers because no one bothers to know the true, righteous me. It might just be that I am different from you. You see... I seek racial equality on a daily basis, but daily...bases are loaded in this unjust society leaving me nowhere to run but back home ... yet we scream "equality." I was taught to love all, but warned that all will not love me...because *I be*...one whose English is often broken. One whose GPA was not above average...and one whose parents never experienced marriage and baby carriages, for those who resemble my sister, are pushed quite early. Up early in the morning I am dressed to impress ready to address a world that looks down on me because I am a minority and the majority rules against me, hence the term: *inequality*.

In equality...

In equality...lies mystery...dating back to our early history. I have yet to see it take its full dictionary meaning...screaming to used to its full potential...but when I pull the credentials on America I see that we have yet to be qualified as the land of the free, home the brave...caved inside of this den of stereotypes on Blacks and Whites, Asian to Hispanics and Puerto Ricans as the quarter seeking to be spent in my pocket says "In God we trust" when it is actually the currency to which we pray. We say equality but how many of us claim to love God yet condemn the crackhead?

In equality lies love, forgiveness and peace, yet we cease to be equal when the spirit of Jim Crow, and the Ku Klux Klan, and the Black Panthers and the Neo-Nazis hunts us all.

What happened to the Martin Luther Kings' and the Gandhis', and the blacks and whites who marched with fingers interlocked protesting the injustices at City Hall? Many fall victim to gunshots as shots gun down black men and white women who lovingly locked lips...when God originally planned for the whole world to be one big interracial relationship. Nations grip hands at peace treaties and summits hoping to come to some kind of agreement but as my knees bent last night I was still praying for the end of war. Plato said that "Only the dead have seen the end of war", and the more I pray...the more I weep...and the more I weep...the more I pray. And the more I think about equality...I say...I have yet to find it.... As I am blinded by inequality. In equality...I see hollowness and unless we see each other as equal...our thoughts of inequality will never produce an equifinality in equality. Black, white, Hispanics, Asian...I love you all the same...I have been named...righteous.

God let us see out brothers and sisters as equal. We need to dwell in equality.

Memoirs of a Queen

Imagination the scene...

A descendant of an unnamed African queen who was doing some sort of neo-tribal dance for the enjoyment of many lustful descendants of unnamed African kings.

She shakes and jiggles her body for monetary compensation...waiting to be paid by the highest bidder.

A litter of men...like dogs, who snarl, grunt and yell" Shake it for me baby!" as she does as requested. Tested by these neo-African judges of tribal dancing, she passes, according to their standards, with flying colors.

Currency decorates the tribal floor, as she is only compensated by the smallest bill of value...one dollar, as one hollers, "You'd better dance for this loot girl!"

Memoirs of a queen...

Hidden shame laces her eyes as she shakes and gyrates, thinking that it has to be more to life than this, but it pays her well...while the moral account that holds the value of her integrity is depleted.

There was the ritual blaring of tribal drums, remixed as the modern day jingles commonly called "booty music." As the paper currency waves in the air, reminiscent of greyhounds chasing the mechanical rabbit in races, she paces towards the money as if it were commanding her to work harder for that which she craves.

The sweat exuding from her magnificent brown skin begins to form as she shakes harder. She gets down on the grassy terrain of the village festivity otherwise known as the club floor as the descendents beg for more...to be taken off.

At first she was merely topless, now she proceeds to display the secret place that gives birth to future kings and queens, which now stands as nothing short of a spectacle for lustful eyes. Her thighs are rubbed and caressed with defiled hands who demand the queen to "Take it all off", but she has been stripped of her pride the minute she stepped into the tribal party.

However, she has to make a living. "It's not like I am a prostitute" she thinks, but when she blinks, it seems, men are always fondling her, and conning her into some sort of distasteful display of intangible affection. Election candidates scream the promises of a better job market and equal opportunities for every man and woman but she never saw those promises come to fruition; post-election.

Memoirs of a queen...

Can one still maintain the dignity and integrity of the likes of a Queen of Sheba or Nefertiti while displaying sacred clitoral regions like a trophy? Like "I Dream of Jeannie", she probably wishes she could blink and be instantly placed into the profession of her choice, but the voice in her head said to "Do what you gotta do."

Some queens do it for the pleasure. Some queens do it for the treasure.

Some queens do it because they ran out of luck.

There is a better way...but who is to say; some probably had no other option.

It was dancing, abortion or adoption.

She probably loved her kids that much.

God please help the queens, who think there is not a better way.

Memoirs of a queen...

A Letter from a Son to a Mother

Woman...you never cease to amaze me...really. From hanging drapes to doing yard work, I search for something you actually can't do...but to no avail.

Sometimes it's hard to tell dad "I love you." It's a masculine thing.

Sometimes it just doesn't quite have that same ring when I tell you "I love you" in the grand scheme of things.

My eyesight sees nobody but you in its scope when I imagine feminine perfection...and your prayers were my protection when my life became the epitome of the prodigal son.

You have always been the logical one. One who could make sense out foolishness and gibberish, and I deliver this poem to you. Before you buy it...you consider the field, and you're kind of like a sleeping pill when I need to chill and relax.

I ask myself, what did I do to deserve a mother of such noble character and intellectual dexterity, and charity and patience and I enter His courts with praise and His gates with Thanksgiving for living another day to say that "I appreciate you."

Even when I was walking with a rebellious stride, I could never hide my conviction from your motherly intuition. You could see the frown masked beneath the smile, and a child in your arms, I know you always envisioned me as.

When it was you I thought I was deceiving...Even when the pride of my premature masculinity was sending me to Bathsheba and Delilah type dwellings...I could hear you telling me, "You know better."

This a letter to tell you that if it had not been for your prayers and supplication above I would probably be drug six feet beneath the Earth's surface. My heart searches for the depths of meaning you are to me. You are a star to me...So far from the ordinary and so far from average and marriage is the only thing that can make you cease from being my number lady. Yet, since I don't have a ring...right now you are my *good thing*.

Your love and compassion is passing the test of time and I ring a chime in my mind every second Sunday in May to relay a message to my spirit man to do something special for you...because *one* mother who is just *two* much equals *three* times a lady.

A lady times heart times soul times peacefulness times integrity times charm times beauty times grace times intelligence times virtue and you are divided by nothing because you are just so whole.

Clothed in the essence of the Virgin Mary...chosen by God to conceive destinies and the best of me is wondering what makes you so poetically unexplainable.

When I was writing this poem for you my love was uncontainable...my pen was unrestrainable.

If my life were Proverbial...you would be the epitome of the 31st chapter verses 10-31. In the New Testament Jesus said, "Son behold thy mother, Mother behold thy son", letting me know one of the last things Christ saw before He saw death was the mother and son union as one. Without Christ and mothers there would be none. Christ's blood running through and your blood running through me made the deal done. We are eternally one.

"Mother, mother there's too many of you crying", and I am trying to understand how a man can sell his own mother's soul for a crack high. But me, I got your back, I'd die for you. It's true. You gave life to me and I will gladly lay down mine for you. To live is Christ and to die is gain and that goes for you too.

You will always be my number 1 "boo." Mother, I love you...

Early Judgment

Osama...you did it. You officially caught America with her underwear down and you took full advantage, and raped her blindfolded and the internal wounds you caused couldn't be fixed with a bandage...or surgery. America became a state of national emergency. I don't defend you. You evil specimen of a man, the epitome of satanic semantics...got this country in a frantic frenzy but those who used to befriend me and were really my enemy now claim to be "patriotically" some kin to me...you know...a United nation? Flags waving everywhere...but a couple of years ago, even minutes before the tragedy; who cared? Who dared to call upon God when everything was going well? I smell hypocrisy. My people have been terrorized for centuries and now you want to mention *me* as your enemy as well...when we are in the same boat? Both looked at as America's foe? America hates you now but they have always taken a dislike towards me...and I award thee with the Certificate of "Bringing America to It Knees" but don't execute another terrorist act please. It sickens me...everybody all "buddy, buddy" with me; when on Sept.10th, they were stereotyping me, and wiping me off as lower class...and 2 blasts into the World Trade and everybody got infected with terrorist AIDS. See, America been raping us with a defective prophylactic and didn't they even know...but the Bible say you reap what you sow. Sir...so will you. You are supposedly hiding in mountainous terrain...Murdering thousands of innocent in Allah's name with no shame...and you will pay. America is still paying and I am saying...it is a blessed curse in a sense. Innocence was lost and guilt remains...filthy stains of blood and evil still saturate ground zero and I found heroes in fireman suits still getting praise, when my heroes only get 28 days.

Yet I found myself crying...weeping at 2am for all the mayhem that this tragedy caused and I paused to say many prayers for consolation and judgment. I have often heard that sin holds no weight; only heavier fleshly consequences so I guess am I just as guilty as you...Just as filthy as you on the inside...when I hide from my righteousness and bless my flesh with its desires. Just as you hired men to carry out your evil fantasies, I fired the voice in my head that was demanding me to not sin. To not bend the rules and justify my acting like a fool...and I am seeing all of these people run to steeples and pray...when all of us in way...are guilty.

It was an early judgment.

Mind of Mine

I am mentally spinning donuts in my mind's parallel dimension as the henchmen try to derail me from my train of thought. The naught optimism is forming full circle, as I no longer see the light in the pathway to my destiny. Momma said there would days like this and noons like this. Nights like this I wish that raindrops would fall on my drought stricken, only good for cotton picking, historically speaking, enslaved mind.

Rewind the tape...I missed the part that states "a mind is a terrible thing to waste", as I think reparations in haste. I taste bitterness in my heart, which makes me psychosomatically affected when I am trying to walk in the pride of a seemingly cursed heritage.

This mind of mine is the kind that is blind to the shine of ice and platinum rhymes.

Thoughts of my kind getting in line with "from twine swinging, Negro spiritual singing King and queens of Africa," demoted to slavery positions...are orphaned at birth.

Where worth is not known by the beholder...labeling is accepted and stamped with the ink of approval and the removal of this ink by ones who try to enlighten the labeled is called, "playa-hatin."

My mind is constantly swinging from thoughts like Tarzan looking for the *Jane* in my people. *Jane* represents purpose...a reason to protect...a reason to uphold a standard...but standard is a victim in our hold-ups...which robs the Black Bank of Morality of its assets and revenue...and who are the criminals?

Minimal minds...

My people are perishing for a lack of knowledge.

My people are lacking for a perished knowledge.

To abolish the slavery in one's mind; one must first recognize the enslaver.

We commonly call this a mirror image.

I hear a lineage of dark hued kings and queens from the grasslands of Nigeria telling me to solely mind the things that will affect the future of their descendants...as the remnants of their dark past are only for educational purposes and not to be repeated. It is to be permanently deleted from the mechanism in our minds that produces excuses.

He/she chooses what will enslave and what will not enslave.

I crave knowledge...even though I sometimes falter in this...

Mind of mine.

Learn.

Unlearn.

The Blood of My Pen

Tick tock tick tock...My mental pendulum is swinging in my brain from left to right, back to left to right...to the depths I write until the blood of my pen stops flowing.

The blood of my pen...

The blood of my pen...

Writing sacrificial verses as I mask the official curses through faith poetry.

I write the pains of my people.

My people...

My steeple in my mind is losing its cross and it seems to have cost me my soul.

Who stole my people's soul?

As the blood of my pen saturates what is recyclable...but I can't recycle my people's time lost.

The black mime tossed his imaginary box out of destiny's window for a tangible closure; for he could no longer front.

I am blunt with my pen strokes, as often times I fail to see hope. Thus the blood of my pen anoints the paper.

I write lyrical leukocytes as the white cells in my poetic stream wither...as the white cells are painted black all too often to imprison the black genius mind.

I am coughing up dead visions as coffin visions terrorize my mind...as too many of my kind are expired.

Who fired Jesus as the King of Kings and gave the Bling of Blings the task of raising my son?

I run from such ignorance but my children fail to distinguish knowledge of self from the glamorization of wealth. Self destruction is played on the radio, backwards, by these neo hip-hoppers...while choppers carry bullet riddled black bodies to the hospital so doctors can make sure that the ink in the "D.O.A." stamp has not dried up.

The blood of my pen is leaking.

The blood of my pen is leaking.

I am seeking and searching while hurting the feelings of my forefathers...as there is more toddlers' body without a visionary.

I pray with persistence.

"Our Father which art in heaven...Hallowed be thy name. Thy Kingdom come. Thy will be done". Yet they kill by gun. They mentally steal my son and brainwash him the modern Euphrates River right near the tree of the knowledge of good and evil. Times have become medieval. People hate each other for no apparent reason. No season but winter prevails in this hell we live in...making it too hot and too cold simultaneously. Aimlessly, it seems, I write sometimes thinking my verses will not even scratch the surface of a revolution because the social pollution is thick.

So quick, I am, to pray.

So quick, I am, to pray.

So quick, I am, to pray that the blood of my pen will cleanse the hearts and souls and mold destinies for our children.

On the Edge of Tomorrow

(For my good friend Michael)

To infinite realms of strength I dive into tomorrow. Sorrows may be waiting but I will come through unscathed. The slave instinct in me is used to hardships and whips on my strong back, but I lack fear...as Psalms 91 is like my palm prints shadow. I have no doubt that tomorrow will throw me low blows beneath my belt and it will release cheap shots...but I weep not in the morning. My tears, biblically stated, have to retire at daybreak.

For the sake of my sons I swim in wisdom streams and dream of the inheritance I shall leave for their seeds. My needs...met. My goals are accomplished although they may only be short term...I am still progressing.

Stressing over what I cannot handle in my earthly strength, I look and see that the length to prayer closet is not far away...as I am praying a day ahead of what may challenge me down the road.

I was told by some to walk alone, as I moan and think about how I shall proceed, thus I read redemptive verses. I resent the verbal curses that say I cannot accomplish tasks by the strength of two minus one but I am an entity of vigor and stamina.

Hammer the nails in the coffin of what was lost; as I toss my visions of sorrow into wide open yesterdays. I am the epitome of a modern day Sampson without the blinded eyes.

I am wise.

I am strong.

I am on the edge of...tomorrow.

Don't Eat Your Destiny

I could imagine ol' George was probably sitting there with a bag full of peanuts and had a thought...*"What can I do with this?"* See, it was more than just a snack...he had a snack with a knack. With that knack he had to compact some facts and ask questions, study his lessons, get suggestions from his colleagues, and roll up his sleeves and not sleep for hours. In his showers were deep thoughts about this small crop...but first...he had to **STOP**...eating...HIS DESTINY.

Rewind the tape back to the date you had that idea on your mental plate and you decided to make a sandwich...with the plan which could have brought you prosperity.

How times have you dined on destiny?

Destine: to set apart for a distinct purpose or end...That means that you can repetitively destine your destiny for doom, in other words your destiny may have been consumed...by you.

It is funny that destiny is never mentioned in the Bible, but the Bible is a book full of various destinies.

Destinies that came forth out of pig sties and eyes that were plucked out due to lust... Do trust...every person has a destiny.

How hungry are you to not eat your destiny?

You don't want to wake up and realize that tomorrow is today and today is a tomorrow waiting to relive yesterday again. Complacency is death's good friend.

Got your fork and your knife, surrounded by your kids and your wife and your life is so unfilled, while your destiny is being is grilled and then eaten, your belly is filled and you are completing another incomplete day.

Don't eat your destiny.

They say that the graveyard is the richest place on Earth because folk went from birth to death, and left their destiny in their last will and testament. Resting it in the coffin right beside them...secrets left unknown. Some of us are dying from an AIDS that is full blown...*Another Incredible Destiny Slaughtered*.... Why? We never bothered to go get it.

Don't get it twisted...destiny is a place you are going. Fate is the result of whichever destiny I choose. Understand...that not even reaching a destiny is a destiny within it self...but it is *that* destiny in which you lose.... So who chews their destiny?

Don't eat your destiny...

Daily I pray, "Father make the streets towards my destiny clear so I don't veer off of some side-road...where some sideshow distraction becomes an attachment to my spirit and I misconstrue that for a destiny shortcut...or a quick scheme to a dream that's ultimately a nightmare. Keep me RIGHT THERE...where you have destined me to be for that moment. Remove these forks and spoons, waiters, and chefs designed by Satan himself that are trying make my destiny my delicacy so they can delicately remove me from my purpose...You see...I am not going to eat my destiny...

I will not eat my destiny...

I will not eat my destiny...

At times we must fast for our destiny...

Have you stopped eating yet?

The Silence of the Lamb

I wonder if He ever once just wanted to scream while the accusers lied about Him. "Kill them Father," He may have thought, but He just remained silent. Violent people spat upon the world's Savior with saliva laced with the flavor of self-righteousness...but He never mumbled a word of revenge. I cringe at the thought of people hitting me and soldiers striping my back with whips with nails attached...hitting the same back that would carry every man, woman and child's sins. Yet, He remained silent.

"Who do you say that I am" was His only phrase, yet no one answered...like cancer...the torment must have ate through His bones. The inner moans...the inner groans of pain and suffering...toughing it out for the sake of a people who loathed the sight of the Word wrapped in skin. They grinned and made mockeries; laughed and gnashed their teeth towards the Man who would bare their grief...but no relief...He died innocent before God...guilty before man.

How filthy were the hands of those who threw rocks and stones and the tones in their voices were saturated with ignorance and to think...the people I am referring to are living in this generation.

Now give that some meditation.

Historic Mirror (Cracked)

I looked in the mirror and stared. I got scared for a minute because I didn't recognize the reflection. I saw the rejection. I saw the polls from the election of "nigga" status I was told I won. I didn't look far enough to see the connection apparatus between me and the One...who created mountains and terrains. I was stained...

Perhaps it was the collapse of my identity that was scarred and maimed through untamed acts of youthful folly that chose to strategically follow me to this very moment of self reflection, and then decided to show its face.

I am confused.

I saw my forefather's shame...The name "slave" was shaved in the back of my afro as my dashiki was laced with bullet holes from racist cops, and hip-hop kept telling me I was next to die from a drive by while I Have A Dream was banned from the radio...it wasn't keeping it real enough.

I am standing in the mirror looking at the reflection of every black man from the beginning of time...and we all favor.

I am confused.

My heart aches of slavery flashbacks, but I got cash stacked from selling crack to my own people, while under the steeple thieves tell me that keeping the man of God well dressed keeps me blessed, but stressed is all I stay...I pray in Ebonics, I am unlearned.

While the cross burned in my front yard...neighborhood MCs took it and used it as a charm on their necklace and told me it was hot...then I got shot...and as I fell I beheld the Klan dapping up the Crips and The Bloods...thanking them for taking on the responsibility of killing me repetitiously...

I am confused.

I watched the slave master as he raped my wife, and made mockeries of her beauty...

I typed in beautiful black women on YouTube and saw clips of pop, lock, and dropping it...all booty.

No brains...just stains of what we were.

I popped in an 8 track and heard 8 tracks about claiming to be a boss, 2 tracks about diamonds that I floss, and 1 track about God helping me be a better person for my son...from a baby momma that I call bitch in rapid succession...

My pilgrimage to Mecca was cut short because 24s was spinning in the wrong direction.

I was more concerned about shining as opposed to learning my lessons.

I became a doctor only to must watch my sister die of HIV given to her by my brother who thinks a rubber is a symbol of weakness...who reaches into his secret closet and pulls out his lover who is the same gender...Send her a message...I tried to heal her through words of awareness...But the carelessness leaves my children without parents.

I am confused.

I was abused by corporate America secret meeting, them deleting my yearly raise because I am not pushing a mop, but graduated at the top of my class, and your subliminal crass remarks do not move me, and I prove we are more than just athletes. They can't stand me.

I am going down the Soul train line doing a tribal dance with my pants hanging below my waist, with a case of Phillie blunts ready for the splitting...weed ready for the hitting...Getting high off my own supply of Miracle Healing Cloths...God is even a pusher now it seems...these dreams are scary, but I claim to be awake.

I am confused.

Who in this Hell am I?

Black.

The Spiritual Slave (Thoughts)

I realize that I still possess the mind of a slave. However I still feel that I am equal to other men in creation. Subconsciously, I still portray the inferiority complex in my words, thoughts, and even my actions. I am therefore acting out the very thing in which I confessing to be free from... a slave mentality.

Daily within my heart and verbal confessions of the mouth, I boast of my standards of excellence, but yet I still settle for that which I feel will suffice for my kind. In my quiet time I had to admit to my inner man that I have made the mediocre acceptable in my standards of life. By doing this I exempt myself from striving for that which the other man labels as *exceptional*. There is a fear that dwells deep within me that was imparted into me hundreds of years ago. Through my struggles, abuse, mistreatment and enslavement I also developed a force that overpowers any mental stronghold. That force is my spirit.

To pinpoint the specifics of my quest I must look at this dilemma from the spiritual aspect at creation.

God created me to look like Him.

God created you to bear His Image.

He created **everyone** in His Likeness.

We were created to subdue and have dominion over the Earth. God's initial plan for man was to have him to be "master" over the earth. The earth was originally subject to serve mankind or to be man's "slave" in a sense. The earth, thus, could not survive without man seeing that God gave him total control over His creation. In my opinion, since there no such thing as sin or negativity yet imparted into the earth, words such as "master", "dominion", and even "slave" were words with positive meanings. However in today's society the always have a negative undertone.

Nevertheless, as a result of Adam's sin, the cycle of slavery and dominion was reversed in an instant.

Suddenly the earth had dominion over man. No longer was the earth not to survive without man, but now man could not survive without the earth. We now have to depend on trees for oxygen when the Word clearly states that God *himself* breathed the breath of life into man.

Along with the cycle reversal of dominion came the element of fear. In the scriptures it states when God gave man dominion that dominion was over the earth in its totality. Including dominion over the fish in the sea, birds of the air and every living creature the moves on the ground. Now, however, we fear many animals: snakes, insects, lions, and even canines. When the slavery was reversed there was also the "fear" element. Thus, whatever we fear we subconsciously are a slave to.

For instance, if you have a fear of snakes you will become enslaved to that part of your mind that triggers the fear of snakes. It will cause (command) you to do abnormal things that will render an all out avoidance of snakes at any cost. Probably at the very sight of snakes, whether in person, in literature or even on the television there will be the sudden impulse to escape its presence by running, turning the page almost ripping it or swiftly changing the channel. All of this happens as a result of the subconscious enslavement to the fear of snakes. When this evolves we forget about our reputation, personality and social status.

Fear has no discretion and often renders embarrassment.

Howard Thurman once wrote, "It is what is actually feared by the rabbit that cannot ultimately escape the hounds." This is meant to say that the rabbit can successfully and repeatedly escape the jaws of its predator. However it will never escape it's fear of being eaten alive. Thus the rabbit is subconsciously a slave to its own fear of death. To put this in a more positive and spiritual connotation, we can take this same truth and relate it to the fear of God. If we fear God (reverence and respect), we will become a slave to Him. Over and over the Bible speaks of the importance of fearing God and keeping His commandments. Though there is the element of fearing God because we realize He has a wrath, I believe that God wants us to fear Him because He loves us and cares so deeply for our daily endeavors. When we become a slave to God and fear Him, we get a sheer delight out of the commands He gives us. This will always lead to victory and a hunger to continue to fear God and keep that which He has charged us to.

So how does this relate to spirituality of enslavement?

It is only when I am imparted with the Spirit of the Living God that I can regain my dominion over the earth's "spiritual" forces; for the scripture states in Ephesians 6:12 that "We wrestle not against flesh and blood, but against principalities, against powers, against the rulers of the darkness of this world and against the *spiritual* wickedness in high places."

The earth, however, is the Lord's and the fullness thereof.

God has given me the power to move earthly situations by His Spirit. This is why we first have to bind it on earth before it can be loosed in heaven. Therefore any physical force opposing me such as racism and social setbacks that are not removed out of my mental realm is because of my own spiritual immaturity.

By nature and the process of birth every living, walking human being is a slave to the earth and sin. However, when I became born again and spirit filled I became a slave to the Spirit of God.

In this process I become the "spiritual slave."

If He commands me to love, I am to love.

If He commands me to forgive, I am to forgive.

If He commands me to give, I am to give.

Therefore His voice and commands, ONLY, I follow.

As the apostle Paul states, " I am no longer a slave to sin, but a slave to Gods law.

By being a slave to God's spirit and His spirit only, I have to begin to see myself as one who receives commands from the Almighty. My voluntary enslavement to God's makes me more than a conqueror in any situation, environment, or statistical placing.

As a result, my race plays no factor in my slavery to the Spirit. My spiritual eyes will only allow me to people by their spirit.

In my African-American heritage, slavery has always played a major role in my history.

Throughout the years, however, the black race, in my opinion, has used slavery as an excuse to not strive for the advancement of our people.

"Mental" slavery has now become the new excuse of the self-enslavement of black Americans. I believe that once we are saved and filled with the Spirit of God we longer have a reason to rely on the crutch of slavery. I agree that there are several forces in today's society that try to hold minorities back as a whole.

However, I also believe that once we strive to really seek after God's heart and develop a deep hunger for a relationship with Him, we will begin to see ourselves as overcomers through His Spirit.

The slaves of old possessed a spirit within them that made them *see* themselves as being free and equal. As a result, there is no such thing as physical enslavement of blacks. The seed was planted and our generation bore the fruit.

Inevitably, we are all a slave to one of two forces; fleshly nature or the Spirit of God.

I must choose to become the spiritual slave.

Therefore I am still a slave; I just have new Master and endless benefits.

I am the spiritual slave.

Sampling

(Hip-Hop, The Classics, History, the Reality)

Hip Hop and the Classics

The other day I was listening to the radio although I really can't deal with this new hip-hop crop. And my mental's central is not that of the mind state of a lyricist who will glorify the rising crime rate. And I guess you can say I "playa-hate" because, to a playa, I just choose not to relate.

These songs about much you get high and who's the next "nigga" to die and then try to balance it out with "I cry, you cry", and these ignorant thong songs...and well, you know, I could on and on.

The songs showcasing the black woman exploitation is getting heavy rotation on the so called "radio for the positive black generation."

However, this particular musical misrepresentation had me in deep meditation. It was like an instant revelation...a spiritual ear and eye opening experience and hearing this made me think historically, realistically and poetically all in the same timeframe. The name of the tune I couldn't recite, but the beat was somewhat tight. I mean the hi-hat and the snare made me bob my head right there but something wasn't quite right.

The instrumentation and the improvisation was cool...but only because it was some sampled "old school."

The piano hook was banging and that old funk was "stanking" and it had me thanking God for the way music used to be. I'm not a dumb brother and lyrics weren't the least bit complex but they confused to vex and confuse me. It was like they were abusing me.

They were raping the mind of my appreciation for the old school artists and the positions that they took. Now I look and see a bamboozled world of non-musical, non-creative borderline blasphemous crooks.

See, it was a re-recorded beat, but these new lyrics were indiscreet...morally obsolete and artistically incomplete. Don't get me wrong I grew up in the hip-hop culture but some of these rappers are like vultures. They are picking apart these peacefully resting rhythm and blues classics to edify their lyrically derogatory theatrics.

They are taking my momma and my daddy's favorite songs that used to glorify the innocence of man and womanhood...when true black love was understood. Back when it was all about platinum chains and iced out wrists...when it was straight honor and respect for the meaning of the fist.

But now my soul is throwing fits and tantrums because we are taking this beautiful music and turning them into ignorance filled ghetto anthems...and we chant them...over and over.

"Range Rover, Range Rover send the next nigga right over"...so he can purchase you and worship you and place even above his own life's destiny. The best of me is wondering why we are taking this beautiful music and making them to glorify weed plants.

And inside my unborn seed chants, "What's going on?" like Marvin. I am starving my musical craving because some hip-hop is enslaving our youth's mind...and times have come where from this musical indiscretion I am fasting and taking permanent rap sabbaticals. I am pushing away my hip-hop plate and resorting to feeding on more jazz, gospel, and classicals.

Music is organized tones and sequences combined to make a continuous composition.

A composition is the act of putting together musical, literary, or artistic work or the final project of something composed. However, even the least musically inclined person knows that most rappers *come posed* as true artists.

History

The darkest element that I dare not label irrelevant is the fact that we are *sampling* some of the ugliest chapters in our black history. As I unfold the facts and mysteries it is killing me what I see.

BLACK PEOPLE...LET ME SADLY MENTION BUT IT MUST BE BROUGHT TO OUR ATTENTION. NOT ONLY ARE WE SAMPLING MUSIC, BUT NOW WE ARE SAMPLING LYNCHINGS!

We have just deleted out the original rope hangers for our time...mixed in a couple of brothers for verses...replaced our microphones for nines, and we call the remix "black on black crime"

We have been placed at number two on God's Billboard chart of commandments broken, "Thou shall not kill", and my brothers are stilling choking, because the nooses wrapped around their necks are too tight. They are being stripped of their life. But the ones hanging them from these ghetto trees that bare strange fruit ain't white.

We got project "P. Diddys" composing realistic murder tracks in our inner cities with no pity and no shame. I can name that tune with no notes...just research your statistical findings and you will see the quotes

Not only are we sampling lynchings but now we are sampling sitting on the back of the bus. And even though Rosa made a fuss...when I look in the back of movies, public transportation, and meeting places all I see in the back is us! It is like we have recreated our own little "colored only" section, so wherever I go...I take the front as my historical repossession.

Men...we are sampling the lustful slave-owners indiscretion. Grown men age 35 dating 17-year-old girls. They are impregnating them and leaving them to fend for themselves in this plantation like world.

Beautiful ebony girl can't you see that you are sampling the concubine? Giving your body up quick to any brother whom will buy you even a fake diamond just as long as it shines. It doesn't even have to be genuine, and all you can say is,

"Oooh girl he so fine", and to his player like tactics you are not even blind. Please let me define...anyone who gives up sex for "doe" is officially a (fill in the blank.)

The Reality

There are so many more I could define, but I am too busy crying sampled tears that my forefathers shed, and as they were whipped and beaten they bled...so I can live my life without imitations of emancipations. But our original creations are trapped in the clutches of ignorance and limitation.

We need to sample some Fredrick Douglas' and some intellectual Nat Turners' if need be. We need to sample some Martins', Marcus', and Malcolms' and strong positive brothers our seeds shall be.

I need Thee, Oh God; to sample my heart that I may be certain that what I am searching for is the moral, spiritual and financial prosperity of my people.

My fathers...

My mothers...

My sisters...

My brothers...

This piece was not written to be entertaining, and not solely about music am I complaining. I am explaining the things that ail my broken historical heart and apart from the obvious we need to be solving this...epidemic sampling.

If your legacy was revisited and sampled; would it be considered a classic, or thrown in the wastebasket?

Dear Teacher

deer teachr,

thannk yu for tha lessin on rol modals. I lernded a hole lott. You had tol me to wach b.e.t. for furrthr reserch and et helpded me a hole lott. Wen I wuz waching it I saww a hole lott of vidios and comec vew. It wuz reaal funy two. They wuz talking abot how bad blak peeples cridet is and howw we always be loudd in tha movie theatar...and they had sed that we don't nevr be on tyme for nuthin. It was reall funy. And then they wuz talkin abot how we always be wuntin to have sexx an how sory the mens wuz and stuf. This ladie wuz on ther and she wuz sayin how she wuld do anythin for a mann if he had give her some mony and she wuz sayin she wuz a femal pemp. She had sumthin abot her baby dadi two. She wuz real funy. Then tis man wuz on ther to and he had sed that he smoke marijuwanna and how wen the polis had stopded him he wuz real hih and he had started laffin at the polis becuz the polis had sed he wuz two hih to be dryvin. I forgit that man name but he wuz funy...he had said that he had droped out of hih scool because his teachers sed he had playd two muchh so he startd tellin jokes to git payed. But then he had sed somthin like, "kids, stay in scool". But he wuz rich, so I thenk I am gonna do whut he had did.

My momma wuz on the telifon so she didn't now dat I wuz watchin tv. See, I usuly be playin my playstaton2 so she thout I wuz doin that so she didn't say noting. Aftar that, thes muzik vidios had came on. It was fat to. This man wuz on ther rapin abot his car and he wuz rapin abot how he wold kil anothr man if he tried to take his munny. He sound lik he wuz mad. But it wuz cool because he sed he was kepin it reel. And then this pritty lady wuz on ther singin abot her nek and her bak. I dednt now whut she wuz talkin about but my moma sed that I wuz two yung to understan. It sond juss like how my moma be talkin wen she be wit her frinds in the livin room whn I be playin my playstaton2. That lady wuz nasty. But I thenk the bestest thing I saw wuz wen tis man wuz on ther and he wuz rappin abot these rems he had on his car. It was fat. He sed that wen his car stop, the rems keeped spinning. I didn't beleeve him but then they had showded it on the vidio and I was like dang I am gong to get som of dem wen I git big. But he was only 18 so thet means I can get sum on dem rems in 5 yers. Afta thet the news had cam on an they wuz talkin abot how a lot of blak men stil gradaute from hih schol and cant red and writ. I am gled thet you take tha tyme wiff me an tell me how whale my riting has impruvd an how you cant wate to see me leave your clas. Plus, they had sed somthin abot how we are packing ot the prisins and jell cells two. Thay had showd som men in jell but thay didn't look as cool as dem rappers so I thenk I am going to rap so I don't go to jell. I thenk that being a rapper is easer than going to jell..all yu hav to do make a goood song and talk abot how yu gruw up in the strets and how you shute peepl. I can do dat. Becuz if you do it an then rap abot it you wont get in trubble. I cant wate to get big. I am gong to be riche. The nuws wuz stil on but thin my moma tol me to get my butt in tha bed. She had sed that I dont need to be wachin all dat nuws abot how bad blak peeples ar. I had fun doin thes projec.

Thenk you teacha,

The studen wifout a rol modal

Commentary on "Dear Teacher

It was brought to my attention that many people might not have quite grasped the total concept of the poem "Dear Teacher." Thus, I will attempt to break down the contents of this writing.

This particular piece illustrates a variety of issues.

The first issue I was trying to portray in this poem was the issue of the role models that the majority of kids have in our lower class areas and even abroad.

I make a conscious effort to try to keep up with what is influencing our youth of today. Thus, I look at what *our* kids look at. This consists of mainly music videos and television in general.

1. The Images on TV

Since this poem is specifically geared towards, but not limited to, the black race, I chose to dissect the programming on *our* so-called television station.

As I watched this programming during the time when most of our children are at home and are awake (between 4pm and 11pm), I made some very interesting observations. (The following is the lineup for only Monday, however the hours for these two particular shows remain consistent throughout the week.)

At 4pm (E.S.T.) there is a music video show that airs from 4pm – 6pm. Immediately following is another music video show that comes on at 6pm until 7:30pm. Already we see that this is three and a half straight hours of music videos.

At ten o'clock, after a movie, a comedy show comes on until eleven o'clock.

Here we have four and a half hours of music videos and comedy in a seven hour period.

If we add that up, that will equal 22.5 hours of music videos and comedy for our children per week!

That is almost equal to our children spending one whole day in front of the television watching this type of programming. I am not saying that all of this programming is bad, but if you take the time to listen; 75% of the lyrics of our popular music is not helping our kids. It glorifies the street life, money, fast cars with big rims, sex, power and living for self ("Gettin' yours").

A great majority of the innuendo on this particular comedy show was not suitable for the mind of a young boy or girl. Adults probably have no problem handling it. For the kids, however, it is a different story. I have personally taken the time to listen to these comics. Some I have found quite entertaining and funny; yet, others are nothing short of a neo- black exploitation performer.

With topics ranging from, but not limited to, sex (any kind imaginable), the enjoyment of drugs (specifically marijuana), alcohol, the problems of black folk i.e., bad credit, our inconsistencies, our accepted tardiness, our rambunctious behavior when wronged, our bad grammar, the lack of motivation by our men, etc., I was very disturbed.

I noticed that many of the female comics were very negative towards the men, except for a few women who showed mad love and support for us. I asked myself what message was this was sending to our children. Here we have all of this negativity and the most that these artists and comedians/comediennes could say was that they were "keeping it real."

Needless to say, there needs to be closer monitoring of what we allow into the ear gates and eye gates of our children. Yes, it matters, tremendously!

2. **The Education System**

Jawanza Kunfuju, author of the book "Countering the
Conspiracy to Destroy Black Boys" said in his book,
"Principals have informed me that they place their "best"
teachers, including men, to maintain order to the most
undisciplined children. This is a Band-Aid approach."

My question is, "How do these kids become undisciplined
in the *upper grades*?" Obviously, some teachers and/or
parents did not take time with them in their lower grades.
Before you think it, I have worked in the school system for
three years and have experienced these things first hand.

I am quite sure you noticed the lack of correct grammar
that was in this piece I tried to display. Me having worked
in the school system for three years as an assistant teacher
(one year in elementary and two years in middle school), I
have seen the cycle of discipline and "putting off" of the
kids; as well as observed many "teacher's lounge
conversations." Particularly in my experiences in middle
school, I noticed the lack of patience in teachers with "at-
risk" children (which are mostly African American
students).

My job at the school was the counselor in the "In School
Suspension" classroom. I must say that I was blessed to
have this position because I had the chance to develop

certain relationships with some students that, to this day, remain.

In this particular position I dealt with what many would call the "problem children."

I would venture to say that one of the most depressing observations I made was that the "problem children" I dealt with were also the same kids who had the most problem functioning on grade level. As I stated earlier, I had many opportunities to talk one on one with these children who, in my opinion, were nothing short of brilliant and bright. However, there has to be a specific development of this brilliance.

We call this process education.

One of the first things I would have the children to do when they were "sentenced" to my class was to have them write out exactly what happened. Needless to say I had some very interesting responses. I have read quite a few papers that were very similar to the poem I wrote, as it relates to its grammatical inconsistencies. Keep in mind these were children on a sixth to eighth grade level. Many times it took me a while to figure out what was being said, but once it was comprehended I realized that these were, by no means, dumb children. Many of these particular children were placed in special education programs such as L.D. (Learning Disabled), B.E.D (Behaviorally Educable

Disabled), and E.M.D. (Emotionally Mentally Disturbed). Statistics say that African American children account for 17% of children in public schools but account for 41% of the children in special education. In addition, 85% of those children are black men. I have always believed that teaching is more than a profession. It is a ministry as well as a calling.

One thing we need to understand is that a great percentage of teachers in our school systems are teaching solely because they could not get a job in the field that they originally majored in.

This is sad, but true. Since this is the case, we are now hiring teachers that are very dissatisfied. First, with themselves for not doing what they think they should be, and second, because they simply never had the desire to teach in the first place. In other words, it is just a paycheck to them. Basically, the schools systems are now hiring anybody with a degree. This inevitably equals lack of patience, lack of love and lack of support for the students.

I observed that many kids who were being promoted were tremendously below grade level. Some of them had trouble with simple addition and the spelling of simple words. That bothered me. Am I advocating the practice of retaining students in mass proportions? No. I am simply questioning the integrity of certain teachers who have the audacity to try and mold a living, breathing child knowing that they have a great impact on their future, but could care less about the child's educational well being. I am not saying that all teachers are bad. I can say that most of the teachers I had were genuinely concerned with my future; most of whom encouraged me to write at an early age.

However, I am not solely blaming the teachers who could care less; I am also, and even more so, holding the parents responsible. When I would ask these kids what was the agenda after school the responses generally stayed consistent from student to student. These activities ranged from going home, watching TV, going outside and playing, going to the local recreation centers and playing ball and a great majority of the responses consisted of playing video games for hours on end. I understand that many of these children resided in single parent homes leaving the mother to work two jobs. However, there are several free afterschool programs for kids who are home alone for a great deal of time after school.

3. The Resolution

The problem is that most of our children are just tolerated instead of properly educated. Shooting basketball after school is not helping our kids excel. We have enough black athletes; some of which still display a lack of discipline even at millionaire status. Of course it will help them to develop social skills, but that alone does not develop a *whole* child. Thus, we have borderline illiterate children who think that just because they have passed certain grades and even have graduated, they are entitled to the same opportunities of those that have buckled down and studied. This, then, leads to rebellion and bitterness on the part of those children who find themselves at a disadvantage at large. Inevitably, most will resort to a life of crime...not, because they were bred as bad children, but because they feel that they have been wronged by the system that governs our lives. In turn they carry a personal vendetta against society as a whole. This is why, I feel, that many of our black men are unbiased as to who they commit a crime against...they feel as if everybody is against them. Unfortunately, since they are usually surrounded by each other, they commit the crimes against one another...which explains the high black on black crime rate.

What are we doing as parents and mentors?

On second thought, who stands as our children's mentors?

Rappers who convey lyrical messages of negativity and street life? Comics who convey the message that is it a laughing matter that black people are in such bad shape? Well, the children have to look for somebody, and as I stated earlier in my dissection of afterschool and evening television programming; TV seems to be the only thing consistent in their lives.

Think on that.

We need to re-evaluate our responsibilities as parents and mentors to a generation who, at times, seems hopeless.

Silent Drum

I am beating my silent drum as my soul moans out a slave like hum. I am trying to send tribal messages by the spirit to my ancestors that something has gone terribly wrong in the neo-village. The pillage and this nationwide off key black harmony is harming me and disarming me of my inner artillery but inwardly I beat and beat...Hoping that the rhythmic patterns created in my soul will permeate through generational curses...and the verses in my heart's song will be heard by African kings and queens of Bible times. I am like a survival mime...trapped inside of a black box on September 11th planes and inner city terrains, but I keep surviving crashes and surviving tribal lashes and with the fight of Cassius, I stand as a man. But I am shackled, trapped inside a black genocidal world of thugs and ghetto killers who slander and steal and sell their soul to platinum gods for ice. Thrice I bang my drum...One for the father, one for the Son, and one for the Spirit that is Holy and You hear it Father then show me and speak audibly to my brothers gone astray. I play polyrhythmic, therapeutic patterns on my drum until my hands are numb. My fingers are blistered, as are my feet; as I am doing rain dances in these ghetto streets...to protect my righteous souls from these hot coals, and this genocidal pot holds my prodigal brothers souls as sacrifices; being lured away by materialistic devices. Brothers lusting for money, sex and status...wanting to push pimp like Caddys, and content with being baby-daddies instead of fathers and it bothers me to see beautiful black mothers in search of tribal festivities instead of properly raising their daughters. These diseased and ignorance infested waters bathes our seeds minds. And I ringing chimes, banging Proverbial rudiments on djembes in the Congo's, Dancing out of my clothes like King David, praying at the top of my lungs, hoping that somebody in the spirit of Africa will hear the sound of my heart's drum and again I ... Hummmmmmmmmm...

I am meditating. I am medicating my hurting soul with spiritual ointments, playing so loud that I override the generational disappointments. I am writing Psalms in poetic hieroglyphics instead of adding to the crime rate statistics. I am chanting Bible verses, hoping that these tribal curses reverses and transforms into millennial blessings but right now I am stressing as I play my silent drum, play my silent drum. Lord hears the rhythm in my blues as I play my silent drum for...You.

Uncherished Womb

Your womb is becoming a graveyard for semen...It sees men day in and day out, and "they in" and "they out"...rotating in shifts within your dock.

Woman hold ragged from years of V.I.P. entrances misconstrued for love and acceptance...freely handing out your goodies to trick or treaters who trick you for the treat in the mid-region of temple...And where is this curse hiding?

Between the handing out of coochie coupons and closing up shop for tampons, your secret garden is opened for the exposure of many...Adjustable to fit various widths and lengths of penile deception...suggesting that "I'm cumming" is the equivalent to "I love you", or "I like you", or merely "I acknowledge the gift", as men sift through your canal with corroded paddles infecting your stream...As your ovarian regions see various legions of seeds deleted by the morning after pill...You peel off, after morning, the remains of last night.

On your back...you lye...lie to self saying, "I just love to sex", knowing that you just sex to love...as Trojan and Lifestyles packets are accentuated by your carpet...only if they are available before sessions.

Clitoral morals buried by his oral fiction of how much he loves you...until the climax ends...buried by his sexual sins... You singe in it's stench of worthlessness.

Mid-20's with the womb of Ethiopian great grandmother who has witnessed the Rites of Passage of the many offspring she has created...as your rite of passage is validated at home after home, belly to belly, and bed after bed...Misled, sister, don't be.

As your legs close, the bank that cashes your reality checks opens and you realize that the stop payment went through...as you were...time after time. And where is the demon that has hexed you? Vagina close to being unsalvageable...

Cherish your womb...

Cherish your womb...

Multitudes of greatness lie within...

Sister...Cherish your womb.

Stereotypes

Pocketbooks were clutched tightly as I walked by them as if they had something that I wanted.

Like I was a haunted possessed spirit from a slave camp that was coming back to get up close and personal reparations.

My meditations were on buying some DVDs and some old school Lps...

Please tell these women that I don't want what they don't offer.

The softer side of me prevailed.

I wanted to yell righteous vulgarities minus the righteous part...but I'm too smart to let my integrity be diminished down to their level of unfinished inner racial stereotype issues.

The review on America's "A Nations United Status"? The saddest it's ever been.

2 thumbs down...

And this is without the clowns in the whites gowns and hoods screaming

"white power!!!"

It's a frightened coward who still sees me as a threat to their perceived superiority.

I relieved my inferiority complex permanently...but yet the social crosses still burn against me.

Me, you fear... Me, you fear.... Me, you fear.

Thinking that I have a spear in my back pocket from my African artifacts collection wanting to punish you, but I'm still being punished.

The question that should be asked is

"Shouldn't I fear you?"

Are you not the ones who are partially responsible for my social setbacks?

But when I set music tracks to vocals to explain my pain, I am labeled racist.

My love basis is a biblical one.

My spiritual gun shoots bullets of historical forgiveness, only wanting my reparations and reciprocity to come in the form of respect and honesty.

I choose to vocalize my pain artistically instead of physically.

Statistically, it says we commit the most crimes.

(the ones that are actually put on records)

That doesn't mean we all have gangster mentalities.

Doesn't mean that we all fall victims to "Stick 'em up" ways of survival.

I'm tribal in my thought patterns like Shaka Zulu

And the Voodoo in my Pimp Cup makes me poetically slap down the tricks of stereotypes.

So pick your stereotype.

Pick your stereotype.

I'm not talking about Panasonic or Sony...

I'm talking about the phony baloney "all homies kill the other homies", Tony Montana protégés thinking that we all sell dope and kill for brighter days.

You think I'm going to destroy the world, or merely your world?

I do want to destroy your world.

Your little world that consists of me being beneath you...

Your little world that consists of me being a grief to you...

You little world that consists of me being a thief to you...

A leaf beneath your tree that bears "Strange Fruit."

I want to poetically tear it from the root with these nouns, adjectives, and verbs to curb your appetite for a world that you think will be alright once it's all White.

At times I get angry...

But like W.E.B Dubois I turn my anger's boiling point down to a simmer.

And the bright light to your stereotypes,

I make a dimmer switch...

So even when you itch

You still can't scratch the Black off.

So back off.

I have a dark intelligence...Which is enlightened by the Light.

So even if you can't see what I'm saying, you can still hear me.

Why do you fear me?

Slave

I am a black man. My eyesight is limited from the pouring social rain and the pain in my black soul is even worse than my physical.

It's like a ritual. Every day I am stared at. I am pushed to the back of the line by others and even my own kind...blind to my abilities because statistically...I am supposed to be dead or incarcerated by age 18, yet life does not owe me a thing.

I am stereotyped. Wiped off as one who is only worth anything when dribbling a basketball as the casket calls my name. My brain is infected by visions of being shot down by brown hands.

Infected with visions of being locked down with cuffed hands and shackled feet...deep in fed time...5 to 9 years. Infinite tears are rolling down my bullwhip-scarred face. I taste the blood of my ancestors.

Slave.

I am a young black male with nails in my innocent hands...like my Daddy...with scales on my eyes. Lies told on me. Eyes rolled at me...execution style.

Profiled...called a "nigger" by the police. The same ones who are supposed to protect and serve push my neck to the curb and brutalize me.

Slave.

You ever wonder what it's like to be a nigger?

Try being *black*.

Slave.

Err

America is walking...Walking with a blindfold...Walking with a blindfold in the dark...Walking with a blindfold in the dark in a strange land.

We are tiptoeing through withering tulips and feeling our way through sins masqueraded as conscious decisions to justify immorality.

Err.

Committing spiritual adultery with mental Delilah's and political Eves with no fig leaves to cover our naked shame before God.

We are Judas-ed.

Hanging ourselves with familiar ropes...like dope to an addict, we are hallucinating off superficiality.

We kiss Jesus' cheek and then speak against He who delivers us from our sins. We are presenting our sin riddled bodies as dead sacrifices, unholy, and helplessly lagging behind even the acceptable...to be exposed secretly before openly, hoping the odor of disobedient acts won't exude from underneath our "In God we trust" masks.

Err.

We have lost touch. We have tossed much garbage from our spirits but we have perfectly the art of fleshly recycling.

Err.

Spur of the moment decision making and breaking rules...

We are treading dangerous pathways with no spiritual compass and our accomplice is flesh. What lies beneath?

Earth tells mysteries as to Adam and Eve like deceptions, questioning if any man can truly be trusted after the Garden of Eden dilemma.

Lies exude from our lips during ritual prayer time. Line for line, God does not hear us either... Neither untruth delves into the depths of Godly like sorrow, for tomorrow God knows we will...err.

As for today, we should opt to not even bend our knees with incessant pleas for forgiveness with hands to repent for what we are planning to do regardless.

We are heartless and simultaneously guilt-ridden, with our guilt hidden and eye to eye contact with the Father is forbidden.

Backslidden....

I do not know if, as a country, we will ever make it into those gates...wear a shiny robe and commune with the disciples of old while walking on the streets of gold. Is there a such thing as "one-fourth" spotless? We got this salvation thing all misconstrued.

God is not pleased with His children.

America...

Err.

Ghetto Prayer Cocoon

My mind is blocked as I am suffering from cocked glock visions, putting incisions on this black soul of mine.

I am standing at the chalk line of a generation gone blind and I am crying.

I want to go back to my cocoon.

I want to go back to my cocoon.

I am a black butterfly and I want to go back to my cocoon.

This soon-to-come Apocalypse got my lips praying.

I am saying to myself, "How long will we grip our nines and ignore the warnings?"

Mornings are not promised but we live as if they are...

Mornings are not promised but we live as if they are...

Donny Hathaway said that tomorrow is made for some, but mornings are not promised, but we live as if they are.

We are living as if a car can carry us to our destiny...

Cars that are fresh, chromed out and sitting on 22s .We have plenty of shoes in the closet...but knowledge is homeless.

We have plenty of fly fashion in the closet but knowledge is homeless.

Is wisdom beginning to write his testament and last will?

We kill a black man...To subtract a black man...To jack a black man...To add to our own greedy hands, which equals sequels to lynching.

Can I mention? Brothers are walking around comatose with their eyes wide shut.

Brothers are walking around comatose with their eyes wide shut.

What the deal?

What the real brothers are saying is strictly being played on the underground circuit.

It is worth it to listen to but dissed is all I get.

Yet, all I get...I give.

I live for my message; yet, I will die for my cause.

I would venture to say that there will be plenty of applause at my funeral but I will probably be eternally weeping in my casket.

My friends will bury me in my basket drenched in six feet of eternal tears.

Here's to my forefather who lost their lives for their wives and seed's freedom.

Do we heed them? The warnings?

Do we heed them brothers? The warnings?

The mourning of too many moms and pops whose sons were gunned down in front of liquor shops and weed spots...

Ghetto blocks, for our kind, are the most common cemetery.

See me bury my big brothers in 6-10 years of federal time...

See me bury my little sisters in premature prostitution for diapers and milk...my newborn nephews are profusely crying...

The shine from the bling-bling is blocking out the lights of our destiny.

Intellectually I try to cope but I can't.

Literarily I try to cope but I can't.

I watch the news and try to cope but I can't.

Thus I chant healing verses from noon to noon. And until I see a change in black life...you can probably find me praying in my ghetto cocoon.

Thought Life

Mentally I am pumping iron so I can give muscle mass to my thought life. This intellectual kinkiness was causing my slave mentality to nap back to its roots so I had to perm my brain. Now I can think straight. Now I can link and contemplate what makes geniuses so common among us, though we can't see beyond the pimp hand that has so systematically slapped us down by the generation. Is it a white man or a black man though? We grow marijuana trees in the backyard of the slave field to puff and keep it real right? Keep it ignorant I say.

I may be caught up in my righteous indignation as I station my train of thought in the reality of what is slaughtering the "would be" infinite black intelligentsia. The Valencia has been squeezed out of the *orange* of our thoughts causing us to recreate Rosewood scenes minus the white man.

Rewrite the plan of attack.

Insight gives us time to act instead of react, but we reenact the trap that was set long ago under burning crosses.

Who is this demon that has hexed us into thinking that we are nothing more than a point guard or a video freak of the week?

I seek answers.

If I were a pimp, I would trick out the spirit of Harriet Tubman so I could infect lustful brothers with the healthy disease of understanding and determination; as I deter my nation from stupidity.

Are you kidding me?

Who was it that invented most things that we now need for day to day survival? A tribal leader's offspring from the grasslands of Nigeria.

Destiny...

Less than we...it is you or I who creates the unfathomable element of brilliance that creativity holds...Yet rolls of money have now become the revolution.

Infected mental contusions have caused us to put Band-Aids over evolving bullet wounds, as our children are hypnotized over these "pull-it" tunes.

"Pull the trigger...."

"Pull the nine out of the trunk of the heavy Chevy...."

"Pull the platinum off of your neck and wrist...."

"Pull the hoe off of the block so you get the money she has made so you can pimp harder...."

Carter G. I Wood son but nobody wants your knowledge anymore. They just want G-notes stacks that they hope will catapult them into millionaire status.

This thug apparatus has them thinking that a bandana makes them invincible.

A sensible approach to the aspect of reasoning is leaving them.

I am seasoning my thoughts with the tang of intellectual oregano so healthy phrases can flow from my grill piece.

Who will release the peace like Dr. King who free styled the "I Have a Dream" portion of his March on Washington speech?

Impeach the player president and elect a revolution compliant client who sees beyond a froze wrist.

A closed fist and civil rights like fight for freedom in the spirit realm to overwhelm the Jesse Helms like attitude. I walk my thoughts in the nude so these dudes can see what I am thinking...with discretion as my thought's lease so this knowledge won't be released before its time...but the time is now.

Think

Many days I just sit and think about what's up with the crime rate...the time it takes to make another brother reach his fate. Mistakes are made...repetition in format...empowerment of all my people; I am for that. Four blacks in fact... two of them them locked up...one is dead... one heeds to the pleas. Fleas got my dawgs itching...scratching the surface of genocide and homicide and in case you haven't checked, black males are quickly rising in the statistics of suicide. And last night I cried because another brother died because a hood rat lied...and a jealous brother blew of his whole left side. His nine was cocked and shot on the MLK block, another one weeping, keeping the cemetery open for moms and pops. Mum's the word for peace parties...151 Bacardi got my brothers acting naughty. And you think we're making progress? Come on brother, not hardly.

Materialistic minds can't see beneath the surface...is it worth this...rapping about gun clapping ...and what your necklaces worth is?

I got a question. Are you really living or just existing? Are you resisting the temptation? Brother we are living in Revelations...and Hell is waiting to add black wood the inferno. Eternal damnation for those who refuse information...Here's the situation. There is no such thing as privacy. Internet browsing is another word for *them* watching me. I see beyond the glitter and gold. What does it profit a man to gain the world and lose his only soul?

The spiritual revolution will not be televised...but you can buy the bootlegged version...so you can look with scaled eyes. Scaled lies weigh a ton. My third eye is blind to reality...but I use my sixth sense so I can see beyond the fallacies.

The mind is a terrible thing to waste...and even though bitterness has a sour taste...we need to take our place. We need to get back what was stolen...not reparations but spiritual meditation.

WE need to think.

WE need to think.

King-Like Dignity

No matter what comes my way this day I must maintain a king-like dignity. People will respect my royalty, for I represent Christ, a child of the most high God. I will walk with my head high today, because the second my head drops in defeat my crown will go crashing to the earth becoming contaminated and defiled. There is no foe, enemy, situation or circumstance that can make me relinquish my spiritual royalty in Jesus.

Unkind words, snide remarks, stereotypical images, evil eyes or attempted social setbacks will not cause me to question my royal inheritance through Christ. I must maintain a king-like dignity. Though my chest is out I will remain humble. A king-like dignity is the ways I choose to respect myself that make others absent from the choice to dishonor me. I walk with a stride reminiscent of the way Adam must have walked when He had total dominion over the earth. Though I don't boast of dominance, I dominate my self-worth. I dominate my self-esteem. I dominate my self-respect. I am more than a conqueror through Christ. Others will ponder over what makes me so different. I see myself as a royal son of God, high enough to reach God but low enough to reach down and help my fellow man up off the grounds of defeat and failure. I resist arrogance, pride and self-centeredness to be that keeper to my brother. I maintain a king-like dignity thus having no other choice but to treat my sisters like the queens that they are. By submitting myself to the King of Kings, The Prince of Peace and The Lord of Lords the royalty runs in my bloodline.

I must maintain a king-like dignity.

Time Stand Still for My Seeds

I would chase a million tomorrows' to catch a glimpse of my seeds in the hereafter. I hear laughter in my mind but time is telling me to move ahead.

Time stands still...

Time still stands...

Stand still time...so I can see my seeds still here after I am deceased.

Generational curses are continuing like clockwork and if the clock works then there is still but time.

Time stand still...

I am daily experiencing my rite of passage...but my right to pass age on down to my sons is ,statistically, a borderline fantasy...as borders line my mind's black box to record the disaster yet to come...Thus I ask for time to stand still.

Purpose gave birth to me; thus I was placed on Earth on purpose, by purpose. My purpose is the mother of my dreams...thus I give time my purpose as collateral...and my purpose in turn replenishes my time lost.

Purpose is the child of destiny...because my destiny gave birth to my purpose...making me destiny's only grandson. I hand one dream to my son making him destiny's great grandson and his son destiny's great-great grandson...Thus meaning my infinite offspring evolve greater and greater as a result of me understanding that I was purposes original embryo.

God gave me this revelation...and I now understand why each generation is labeled greater than the seed preceding.

I heed to the reading...I plead to time needing him to understand that I finally grasped the concept that I live for my sons...and not for selfish gain. I felt this pain in my stomach...not realizing that it was my unborn seeds telling me that I was wasting...his time and not mine. I was crying his tears...I was living his fears...I was wasting his years. It appears that it all began with Christ. John 14:12 says that because I believe on Him, I shall do greater works than He...because He goeth back to His father. Thus when I go back to my father and when I am dead and gone my own seeds shall build on what I left behind. This defines my son as greater than I. This is why my son's son is my grandson because he was destined to be grander than I. And his son is my great grandson because he should be greater. A generation later comes my great grand because he is than two times more grand...Understand? My self...I know. My seeds...I sow for the strength of my sons and daughters, borders on me having nothing that I may see the prosperity of my offspring. Off summer clouds I brainstorm thoughts as to how to get my brothers off the block and off the stock market and target themselves as *biological* trendsetters...as birds of a feather flock together thus my sons soar on the wings of eagles. On my mind's counter the clock is wise that I may think back to the mistakes I made so my sons won't become prodigal like I did. The grid shows that we are falling short of what was biblically ordained. Like Cane, we are killing our brothers for envy. Lord, send me to the gardens that I may poetically water my brother's hearts hardened. My seeds are depending on me void of tangible hands, in my bosom, waiting on me to dismantle plans of yet another generational curse. This inspirational verse was written with a pen on tear soaked paper and not later but now is the time to produce life for my seeds. Break these curses...oh God...from my seed...break these curses. Time stand still...for my seeds.

The Covenant of a Father

"I cannot think of any need in childhood as strong as the need for a father's protection."

Sigmund Freud

"It is easier for a father to have children than for children to have a real father."

Pope John XXIII

The role of the father...

The father who, from a newborn to a toddler, from a toddler to an adolescent teaches lessons, stressing the importance of manhood, what a man should and should not do...who does not misconstrue correction for abuse, and loves his seed unconditionally.

Traditionally, the father is the provider of the home. He makes sure the table is full and the bills are paid, and the foundation is laid and the pathway is paved for his offspring's future.

The voice of the father...

All he had to say was, "Boy if I got to tell you one more time", and instantly you fell in line...

A father...Strong.

A father...Stern.

A father...commanding respect by his character alone.

What happened to the fathers?

Now father has been replaced with baby daddy. Sadly, children are suffering due to a lack of paternal guidance and bitter mothers who smother their sons with gifts to shift the need of a father and slaughters the morale of their kids unknowingly.

The duties of a father has been substituted with a polluted view of who runs a household, as teenagers are told to watch their siblings at wee hours of the night while mother is out 2 stepping at the local disco...with no father to be found and the sound of another dysfunctional family becomes all too audible.

The family has lost its father.

The family has lost its father.

Young boys are looking for daddy in obscene rappers and the local drug dealer.

Young girls are searching for daddy through raising up their skirt to conceal the hurt...being made into a woman before they have a chance to be a little girl...our world is suffering because too many fathers' faces are traces of mystery.

Paul told Young Timothy that a man who does not take care of his family is worse than an infidel. An infidel is a person void of faith...a non-believer, a griever of God's powers...a devourer of the covenant.

Mugging their sons of their healing dealing with pride and being irresponsible with it, treating their children like a conjugal visit...fertilizing the seed and not wanting to deal with it...

The covenant has been broken.

The covenant of a father...

The father that prays with and for his family...

The covenant of a father...

A father who worships God through his disciplined life...who loves his wife in front of his children, building the foundation of love through actions...

Practicing what he preaches, breaches contracts of lack and stacks for years to come...Who molds his son...comforts his daughter, understands that God's order is not a dictatorship but a partnership.

The covenant of a father needs to be revealed...The old contract needs to be repealed.

Resealed with the blood of Christ...Fatherhood consists of sacrifice.

The covenant of a father...

Love.

Blind to Reality

I would rather be blind and see than to see and be blind...being mindful of a covenant that was cut long ago. A covenant of promise...A covenant of blood that was sealed on the old rugged. Gold nugget promises, though, got my people praying to platinum calves and half of us, less than actually, are factually prepared for the apocalyptic age. The stage is set, met by immorality and fallacies of immortality, as the modern day cocks are crowing three times three times infinite delusions of trust, thus leaving us the subjects of Peter like denials...screaming, "I don't know me!" "I don't know me!", as the savior of our inner righteousness is nailed to an unjust tree in our people's minds on Golgotha hills renamed ignorance.

Blind to reality.

I would rather be deaf and hear than to hear and be deaf. He left the right path but wrong is known as equal rights in some scenarios and beliefs, as thieves are robbing us blind but we never peripherally saw what was slipping in because we were so focused on getting mines...or ours.

Devours the man...

Devours the woman...

Devours the innocent one who sleeps in yet to be discovered eggs in ovarian regions. Legions of demons attack the seed, with the aftermath of the wrath not discovered until he or she is in a position to lead other seeds which leads to generation after generation contemplating insanity due to a curse that was never reversed but rehearsed, birth after birth after birth, and where worth is not known; self-hate is inevitable.

Schedule the next execution...I hear its gothic, backbeat pianissimo when it comes. It hums bling bling tunes to young ear gates, and here waits the next devil...ready to infiltrate minds of brilliant lads whose dads are represented on TV with wheels that keep spinning when their crack mobile stops.

Who got the props?

Satan is the prince of the air.

I ain't never scared, but I fear those who fear who knowledge.

Who fear dying old and poor, over living shook, young and rich, and the ditch dug is by self for wealth dreams and C.R.E.A.M. schemes and streams of materialism is made up by the great lakes of what our slave parents and beyond didn't have.

Laugh if you will...as it resembles the enemy's historic groan in tone...and I'll continue to moan like my forefathers and mothers...who cried for the freedom of those who came after their demise. The eyes are for seeing ahead not behind...so be blind if you have to...to reality.

Commentary on "Blind to Reality"

"I would rather be blind and see than to see and be blind."

This first sentence is pretty self-explanatory. It basically says that it is better to see what is going on mentally and not see physically than to see what is going physically and not see mentally, socially, etc.

"...be mindful of a covenant that was cut long ago, a covenant of promise. A covenant that was sealed on a cross that was old and rugged."

This particular statement reflects the covenant that was sealed when Jesus Christ died on the cross for our sins. This particular covenant promises the forgiveness of sins and the removal of various curses from the lives of those who believe on Jesus Christ.

"Gold nugget promises though got my people praying to platinum calves..."

Gold nugget promises in that particular text represents anything materialistic that keeps our people in bondage. The promises represent the fallacies of quick money, fame and fortune that have so many of us searching for prosperity the wrong way. Platinum calves represent two things. The platinum is meant to represent the modern day glamorization of the element platinum that is represented and worshipped in our songs and on our videos. The calf symbolizes the Old Testament biblical story in which the children of Israel had made as a false god in which they worshipped. Thus, in order to mix the two, I simply made the calf platinum to symbolize that the calves (or gods) we now worship are platinum. This is to say that we still have the same spirit as the children of Israel who forsake God for material things.

"...and half us of, less than actually, are factually prepared for the Apocalyptic age."

This statement ties into the sentence preceding it. What I was basically saying here was because some of us are so wrapped up in the material; we have totally disregarded the fact that the end times are upon us. When I say "less than actually", I was simply saying that there are many people who fit this category. If one is prepared for something, he must first know the facts. This includes: lawyers, doctors, preachers and even the common man. One must know and be aware of FACTS. Many of us do not know the facts and we are basically going off of what somebody else says, or even worse, choose to be ignorant of them.

"The stage is set. Met be immorality and fallacies of immortality..."

The stage represents the world as a whole. I view life as a stage to perform on. The world is full of people who are filled with immorality: sexual immorality, financial immorality, etc. The stage, as I said, represents the world. The enemy (satan) is responsible for setting the current stage (state of the world). He has filled us with this immorality. Also, he has hexed many people into thinking like they are immortal (incapable of dying). Poetically, I also used immortality as a means of expressing the fact that many people live as if there is no judgment. I carefully labeled this a fallacy because many people are deceived into believing that this is, in fact, true.

"...as the modern day cocks are crowing three times three times three times infinite delusions of trust, thus leaving us

the subject of Peter like denials screaming, "I don't know me, I don't know me..."

This is a very complex and thought provoking statement. The modern day cocks (roosters) represent the warning signs of destruction. In the Bible it states that when Peter denied Jesus, the cock would crow.

Let's start here. As I previously stated, the modern day cocks represent the warning signs of destruction. The warnings include, but are not limited to, pestilence (widespread diseases), wars, plaques, etc. While these cocks are crowing (three times three times three represents endlessly) we are stagnated by infinite delusions of trust. Therefore, because we do not trust in the Word of God, which gives one insight as to what is happening in the end times, we are screaming, "I don't know me", the same way Peter screamed, "I don't know Jesus." Knowledge of self will always give one insight because he would have first believed in his or her ability to comprehend end times as based on the Word. Yet, because we are so wrapped up self and the misconception of self-advancement, we are subconsciously denying ourselves the right to take heed of these warnings. This is also meant to say that many of us are still denying Christ, which also can be translated as saying, "I don't know me", because Christ is a direct reflection of who we are once we are redeemed from the curse.

"...as the Savior of our inner righteousness is nailed to an unjust tree, in our people's minds on Golgotha hills renamed ignorance. I want to be blind to reality."

This particular verse is the defining point of the previous verse. It simply states that because we have denied ourselves and have denied Christ...we are subconsciously killing the righteousness that lies within us. The unjust tree represents the fact that Jesus was wrongfully executed; as are though who choose to deny Christ and themselves. One might ask...Why is this considered by you to be unjust? The reason I labeled it unjust is because we don't have to die (spiritually) like this but we do anyway; just as Jesus did not have to die but He willfully did. WE are wrongfully killing our spirituality, which in a way, is unjust to our own wellbeing. However, Jesus died knowing that His death would save the world. Our spiritual deaths, however, are meaningless because we are dying as a result of ignorance. WE are dying on the Golgotha hill(the hill that Jesus died on) that has been renamed, ignorance. The Bible states, "My people are destroyed for a lack of knowledge." Blind to

Reality in this verse is basically saying, "I really don't want to believe that this is happening, but it is.

"I would rather be deaf and hear, than to hear and be deaf."

This statement has the same definition is the first statement in the piece. I was just using a different physical sense, i.e. hearing, smelling, tasting, seeing, etc.

"He left the right path but wrong is now known as equal rights in some scenarios and beliefs..."

"He" refers to Christ. When Christ died He relayed to the disciples (and the world) that He would leave a comforter which is the Holy Ghost. The Holy Ghost directs paths and gives us warnings and insight various situations. In other words, He left us guidelines (the Word) to live by and to govern ourselves accordingly, i.e. rules, spiritual laws. However, wrong is now known as equal rights in some scenarios. In this particular statement, I was indirectly referring to things that we accept as a nation that we know to be wrong, yet label as equal rights, i.e., homosexuality, same sex marriages, etc. These things are strategically labeled "wrong" in the Word of God, yet we have undermined God's law and labeled them okay. There have been laws passed in certain states that approve of same sex marriages, when the Bible clearly states to "Be fruitful and multiply." Anyone knows that two people of the same sex cannot multiply. In case anyone is wondering who may be reading this; this particular verse was a direct blow to same sex marriages and the curse of homosexuality in America. It is clear that God has a problem with homosexuality and labeled it an "abomination" against Him. The biblical story of Sodom and Gomorrah proves this fact.

"...as thieves are robbing us blind, but we never saw what was peripherally slipping in because we were so focused on getting mine; or ours..."

The imagery "thieves" used in this text represents the things, people or laws that indirectly affect us that will alter the nation or world. One may ask, "What are we getting robbed of?" I feel as if we are getting robed of our rights as humans, and how certain laws passed (homosexual marriages) indirectly affect us. When a law is passed that homosexuals can marry, to me, this is saying that homosexuals are just as moral as I am. This is a false statement. No matter how people want to argue this point, if God labels something as an "abomination" to Him, something is definitely wrong with that person. I'm not saying that these people need to be exiled or put away from the rest of the world; all I am saying is that they need healing. God loves then just as much as He loves me. God never ordained, in His Word, the marriage of people of the same sex. Yet, we as a country have "ordained" this in a sense, which is direct and blatant disrespect to the Written Word of God. This will definitely affect every man. I was listening to the news and I heard it stated on Christian talk that, in Canada, if a person is found in a public place talking against homosexuality, they can be arrested. The Canadian officials consider this "posing a threat" to the homosexual community. I feel as if this can eventually lead to the same thing happening in the United States. So how does this not affect every man? However, getting back to the verse, we are so focused on getting on attaining material things that we do not see what is so blatantly happening to our nation and world. This defines the second part of this verse. I have often heard people say that they choose not to look at the news because it never has anything good to say. I feel that we should all watch the news (especially African Americans) to know and be aware of what is happening around us. True, there is not really that much good news but one should always stay abreast to what is happening in the nation that make rules and laws that will, in some way, affect you and your family.

"...devours the man...devours the woman.....devours the innocent one who sleeps in yet to be discovered eggs in ovarian regions."

This verse goes back and clarifies my previous point. These things that are happening will affect everyone. And if these warnings are not heeded, they could devour a person. This is not meant to say that they will necessarily die; but it is saying that one can be devoured financially, physically, spiritually, socially, etc. These things, if the person does not take proper precaution, can also affect the children will who be born under these same rules. These children are innocent and when they are birthed into this world of injustice and confusion they will be victims too because his or her parents did not take the time to adequately prepare for the detrimental situations.

"...legions of demons attack the seeds; with the aftermath of the wrath not discovered until he or she is in a position to lead other seeds..."

Demonic forces prey on the ignorant. That is why God says that His people are destroyed for a lack of knowledge. Since God has all power and even gives demons permission to destroy, then that tells me that God is warning His people before He sends destruction. This is very clear. This verse basically breaks down the cycle of generational curses. Demons will attack seeds at birth and haunt them until the curse is broken off of their lives. In a lot of cases a person does realize that there is a curse on his/her life until he or she sees it begin to play out in the lives of their children.

There were many things that I did that I did not quite understand why I dealt with them until I found out that my father dealt with the same thing. This is what I mean when I say, "With the aftermath of the wrath not discovered until he or she is in a position to lead other seeds." Many people do not realize that they deal with their father's or mother's demons until they are in a position to lead a household or other people. I feel like this is a strategic move by the enemy in order to affect or infect, if I may, generations of people.

"...which leads to generation after generation contemplating insanity. It was a curse that was never reversed but rehearsed, birth after birth after birth. And

where worth is not known, self hate is inevitable. Blind to reality..."

This verse finalizes my previous verse. As one gets older (I am saying this out of personal experience), one will begin to question his or her own sanity as a result of doing things that he or she knows is not productive or even self-destructive even. This is simply because this curse that has probably been going on for generations was never broken off of his or her life. If a person was never validated as a child by his or her parents as a child, or never told the consequences of ignorance; he or she will more than likely do things that he or she knows will be detrimental. However, because he or she was not told that these things were wrong, they will have to learn the hard way. You ever noticed that when you tell a child not to touch a hot oven but never tell them why not to; they wil touch it anyway? This is because they were not told the consequences of touching the stove. Inevitably, they will get burned, but yet and still continue to, on occasion, touch the stove knowing the consequences. This is the same with generational curses. One does not understand why he or she continues to do certain things that they know is a doorway to a slow destruction. Somewhere in their life they were never validated or told their self worth. This is because the parents that preceded them were not told either... and so forth and so on. If a person is continually doing something that is self destructive; somewhere in their life they were adequately told they true worth. They were not told the preciousness of their temples (bodies), and somewhere deep beneath the surface, there is a small element of self hate that is not noticed mentally but is validated by the things in which he or she does.

"Schedule the next execution. I hear its gothic, backbeat, pianissimo when it comes. It hums bling-tunes to young ear gates...and here waits the next devil, ready to infiltrate the minds of brilliant lads whose dads are represented on the television with wheels that keep spinning when their crackmobile stops. Who got the props? Satan is the prince of the air."

The particular verse refers to the impact that negative hip-hop is having on our young children's minds. When I refer to "execution" I am talking about an abstract execution, i.e., mental execution, moral execution, etc. The gothic (sinister, evil) backbeat (breakbeats, TR-808's drum beats, crunk) pianissimo (low tone, poetically speaking underhanded) when it comes (on the radio, on the CD's, and videos). When I refer to bling-bling, tunes I am referring to the onslaught of the bling-bling, platinum chain, iced out references in our music. The "next devil" in the text refers to the enemy called ignorance. Ignorance infiltrates the minds of these brilliant lads. I say brilliant simply because (contrary to popular belief) young black males are among the most intelligent class of humans. I taught in the school system for 3 years and dealt mostly with "at-risk" or "labeled" students. In one particular class, a class that was labeled B.E.D. (Behaviorally Educable Disabled), I taught 4th and 5th grade students, all black males besides two, lessons that were on an 8th grade level. They were acing spelling tests with words containing approximately 10 to 11 or more letters. Even though these kids were labeled, they had their minds challenged and succeeded. However, these same kids are having their minds infected by the images on television. The reference to "dads" in this particular verse was a direct reflection to the single parent black homes that most of our young men have to deal with. They are being raised by their mothers and a lot of times, the only images they have of a "successful" black men are the same men who encourage them to "keep it real", "keep it crunk", "get high", "throw yo hood up", etc. Ten the question is asked, "Who got the props?" (popular song by hip-hop group Black Moon) The answer is very simple, "Satan is the prince of the air", (Ephesians 2:2). The reason I say this is simply because behind everything that is not God-like, satan is to blame.

"I ain't never scared, but I fear those who fear knowledge...who fear dying old poor, and happy living shook young and rich and a ditch is dug by self for wealth dreams and c.r.e.a.m. schemes..."

Popular "dirty south" rapper, Bonecrusher made a very catchy club anthem entitled, "Neva Scared." In this song he boasts about how nothing or anyone scares him. The hook of the song, however, is one that perplexes me. It states, "Outside of the club and he think I'm a punk. So I go to the heavy Chevy and "pop the trunk". I told...I ain't neva scared." The term "pop the trunk" means to go the trunk of your car and get your "heavy artillery", i.e. guns, whatever. This was an indirect "diss" to this song that was made clear in the next sentence. In the very next statement I make a very abstract yet clear point..."I fear those who fear knowledge." This is saying that I am man who, like Bonecrusher, is not afraid of another human being. However, people who fear or evade knowledge are a direct threat to me. If someone fears knowledge and have not a craving for the truth; they put fear in me. Not a direct fear in me for them but a fear that they will corrupt someone else with their intellectual evasiveness. These people are usually ones who rather live the fast, death stricken life,

(Living shook, young and rich), as opposed to living to become old, poor, yet happy. This verse also makes an indirect reference to how the material things usually enslave my people. This leads me to the next verse.

"A ditch is dug by self for wealth dreams and c.r.e.a.m. schemes..."

Black people are, in my opinion, the most spiritual race of people on the planet. We have overcome the injustices of slavery and racism by a devout belief in the power of God. We sang freedom songs during slave plights, and had peaceful marches during civil rights struggles and one of our most powerful and influential people, Dr. King, was a devout Christian, pastor and spiritual leader. However, now it seems that we have been overtaken by this trend of being validated by material treasures. Here again, I blame this trend on the media and its portrayal of our race. Also, I have to also put a significant amount of blame on our own portrayal of each other. I believe that there always has to some sort of spiritual base for progress of a people, race, or individual. The "ditch that is dug" is the ditch that one digs as a result of pursuing material success that sometimes involves that the alienation of his or her morals, family and spirituality.

"And streams of materialism is made up by the Great Lakes of what our slave parents and beyond didn't have."

I overheard a conversation in which an older black woman was talking about why the younger generation is so material. She said that because a lot of us grew seeing our parents struggle and our parent's parents struggle...they feel to the need to compensate for that by achieving material status. I want you to recognize and pay close attention to the two words that are used in the verse: "streams and Great Lakes." We have (my generation) only have "streams of materialism" as opposed to the "Great Lakes" of what our slave parents and beyond didn't have. As we all know, there is a vast difference between "streams" and "Great Lakes." The reason I used this analogy is because I firmly believe that we will never be able to compensate for what our forefathers went through with our material things. I honestly don't believe that when an older black gentleman looks at television and sees the "bling-blingers", and the "playas" and the Cash Money Millionaires that he feels a sense of accomplishment being played out through the younger generation as a result of his struggles and fights. I DO NOT believe that when someone like Rosa Parks looks at how we act today, she feel likes her fight was worth it. Do you believe that they are proud of us when we demean our women, wear flashy jewelry and rap about crack profits in our songs and videos? No!!! That is why I say we have "streams" of materialism and our strong forefathers and mothers had "Great Lakes" of lack.

"Laugh if you will; as it resembles the enemy's historic groan in tone. And I will continue to moan like my forefathers and mothers who died for the freedom of those who came after their demise. The eyes are for seeing ahead and not behind to be blind, if you have to, to reality."

This last verse is basically my closing statement and prayer. "Laugh if you will" refers to the people who may read this and think that I am extreme, irate, or even foolish for my philosophy on matters. I have often been told that I think too much or that I take issues too far, and quite often I am laughed at. The enemy is this verse refers to the people who are enslaved, stereotyped, used and abused us in times of old. That is why the laugh has a "historic groan in tone." Nevertheless, while people are laughing at talking negatively about my stance on issues, I will continue to moan (pray, have faith in us, meditate, educate, enlighten) like my forefathers and mothers who cried (struggled, fought, were beaten) for the freedom of those who came after their demise (death). In other words, I want to have the same fight, faith, compassion, love and integrity of my forefathers who died so that we can be free. I feel if we all have that same compassion and vision, we will better off as a people. The eyes are for seeing ahead and not behind. In other words, look to the future. So be blind, if you have to, to what is destroying our people...not as a means of ignoring what is going on...but acknowledging it...taking the proper steps to correct it and then move on.

Step Your Game Up: November 4, 2008

Collectively, our games were forced to step up...

Next up to the plate to create pathways for our families...is us.

Thank Barack.

Thank the Rock.

The reciprocity of Simon of Cyrene was seen on all our TV screens and the screams of "we can't do it" were instantly silenced.

Now the excuses are useless. The nooses we used to set for each other are now covered with *Obama '08* stickers and posters...I can't leave you hanging no more, I have to hold you closer.

I have to hold you more accountable and encourage you to overcome that which is deemed insurmountable.

I need you to do the same, thus our destinies can be renamed...accomplished.

I'll tell you and you tell me to...

Step your game up.

Step your name up to being capitalized at all times from now on...we are forced to be proper nouns...

Now forced to drape our women in the most proper gowns...

No more "hand-me-downs", social and emotional letdowns, and discount consignment shop tiaras and crowns...

We epitomize kingship from this point on, no longer paupers now...we are rich.

Can bitch still be used to confuse our sons as the namesake of our first ladies?

Shall we still neglect our babies?

Will we now think twice before overlooking "Keisha" for "Katie?"

Not racist by any means...but the scene of a shapely Michelle will fit so well when we tell our grandchildren that "our" first First Lady was a real "sista."

Let's get real mister...

Step your game up.

The whole dynamic of being a brother has now shifted.

We have long been gifted...But now our consciousness has been lifted to another plateau...a different dimension...an elevated plane...Our brains now have a "priority" sticker placed on them...and our reality is no longer grim.

Thank Barack.

Thank the Rock.

The shanks and glocks that we used to destroy us should now implore us to think twice before they are used to take a life...A black one at that.

Shall we still rap about the fallacious machismo of a thug nigga, when decades ago they drug "niggas" away from the voting booths to cast of a ballot of truth, or shall the youth continue to harmonize ballads of drug niggas who "make it do what it do?"

Will Tony Montana be rightfully replaced by Barack Obama as our young men's vision of success?

Shall we still stress that dress is more important than clothing our son's minds with the knowledge of the time when we were seen as three-fifths of a gift?

Shall we still sift through life with dreams of reaching "baller" status, or will the apparatus of change rearrange our though pattern?

Shall we still settle for being seen as more hyper-sexual than intellectual?

Will we now stop exchanging monetary compensation for subliminal black-facing?

Shall we still glorify the *pimpification* of the black nation? Will we still be trophy-casing our women as showpieces and not masterpieces, while the Master pieces together a creation of what the world thought to be a figment of blacks' imagination...A man running the White House with dark pigmentation?

Now, my brother...I urge you to...

Step *your* game up.

He was the underdog too.

Step *your* game up.

A single mother raised him too.

Step *your* game up.

His father was nothing more than a stranger too.

Step *your* game up.

They dogged him to the dirt too.

Step *your* game up.

They tried to use his own race against him too.

Step *your* game up.

They called him a nigger too.

Step *your* game up.

He always kept his cool. Can you?

Step *your* game up.

I could imagine the nights where the inner fights sent him on flights where the heights of seeing common ground were seemingly impossible.

He remained steadfast...and the last was named first.

The last hearse carrying the dying morale of black men ran out of gas and was refueled with high octane, put in a different lane, and renamed the Midnight Train to the Promised Land.

Pay your fare and let's get there; brother.

Step your game up.

Thank Barack.

But more importantly, thank the Rock.

Philippians 4:13

Slave Ship Scene-Take 2001

This world I am living in is but a slave ship scene. This world I live in is but a slave ship scene. This world I live in is but a slave ship scene. The same old routine...I mean, it's obvious. Black people...supposed to kings and queens, yet enslaved by material things and "bling- blings" which sings to the mind of a generation of "niggas" and "macks" that lack historical understanding. Demanding that we be treated like first class citizens when some of us still are still living in a whole body with only three fifths of a moral being. I am seeing a ship full of brothers, otherwise known as the "block niggas", with cocked triggers taking the place of bullwhips. Chips on their shoulders cause them to brutalize with subconscious green eyes...despising one another for no reason other than, "He looked at me the wrong way." I find myself crowded...locked down at the bottom of the boat...row by row with crackheads and dope dealers, corrupt cops, and liquor shops, and my moms and pops who are barely making it. Here the stench of decaying flesh permeates my interior sanctuary and the scene is scary. I am surrounded by various pieces of artwork known as black bodies...which have now become disease infected, drug injected veins, and platinum chains are like yokes around the necks of the slaves on the bottom deck of this ship called the black community. Community...a common unity? The only element of a union I envision is the decision to stay shackled by stereotypes and pipe dreams of making a killing inside the ship. In other words, selling crack on the block in the ghettos is like slaves selling other slaves life rafts with holes. We got each other hallucinating about being free, all while tacking on another name to the list of black casualties, now even being able to see through the fallacies. Our lips quote the verses of hip hoppers who infect our children's mind with these carnal monologues and ghetto chants...and body ink logos of weed plants to advance a false sense of self -esteem. I dream of a day when my people realize that some of these meaningless tattoos were the same methods slaveowners used to brand and label us as strong or weak, sick or a wealth of health. Some stereotypes we make for ourselves. It should be a sin some of the things we do to fit in. The contamination of our pigmentation that is permanently etched into our bodies and souls...and infinitely identify with our character that will still label us once we get old. With this cold reality I wrestle, but the truth is many of my brothers are going to die on this vessel. God, remove these scales from our eyes...and as much as I don't to live in this reality...the sinking of this ship would be genocide. Look closely at our ghettos and projects. Welfare checks and a living that is government aided is nothing but a masqueraded version of the vessels that used to transport our forefathers. Supplying us with just enough to survive and barely enough necessities to stay alive. The system never strives to encourage the black family to get up out the hood because they own it. All they did was clone it...because I am confident that slave owners never gave slaves a life raft. Add up the math and you will see that it has never been equal, just a sequel now labeled "low income" housing. But some of us can't see...we are too busy Internet browsing. Can't you see it? It is clear as ocean streams the things they are doing...Screwing us with no remorse...The voice of my historical intellect puts in check the underlying conspiracy to keep us locked up all together like they did on the voyages to bring us to America The Beautiful. My knees nightly bend in hopes that my people are awaken...shaken up and motivated and educated as to what is so blatantly executed right before our eyes. Forgive us God for our ignorance.

We are still getting high off of this evil called crack and weed and it is making my heart bleed black blood. I am waddling in this mud and the rainstorms of mis-education is drowning our liberation and flooding the ship which is slowly but surely sinking. I am thinking of ways to plug the cracks but I am locked down...and we are bound by a full blown ignorance. I guess the reality check is when my people are once again shackled to the deck and stripped of every right they possess. I am stressed...barely holding back tears as I address this problem to my brothers...who are too busy passing around the dutch and in turn label me a "nigga" that thinks too much. I am in touch with my historical father's spirit trying to solve the real issue. I hold my brother's hand that he may understand that if we jump of this ship together to weather the sea of freedom and mental emancipation...I am going down with you.

The world I live in is but a slave ship scene.

The Church Rush

The Saul in us has yet to be converted into Apostle status. The saddest of church times is now...where we condemn and mentally murder those who are not like us. They spite us because of our "holier than thou" façade and our Botox shots of self- righteousness...trying to hide what can't be hid...the closet evidence of religious wrinkles. Our songs and dances are saturated with the stains of what we are "pre" and "post" services...trying to be passed off as perfection's mirror image but the glass is cracked. In fact, I will venture to say that some of us only know *of* Jesus and don't really commune with Him. This means the admitting of mistakes and flesh acts, setbacks and faults. However, we are caught in the church lottery of *"name it and claim it"* cover-ups when a *message* is what we really need. Heed to the Biblical warnings...the last days where men will be carried away by their own lusts. The last days where the rush for fortune and fame will be deceptively named as seeking the favor of God and not what it really is...greed. We need revival and knowledge, but what we want is the big check and the cottage that is filled with the material treasures and the pleasure of telling the sinner man..."This is what I got for being saved." But I wonder why many of us don't get the blessings in 30 days? And the wealth in many ways...and the houses on the hill and the thrill of pushing the Bentley with chrome wheels; obviously something is not right. Quite wrong perhaps... The claps of hands are thunderous as the pastor proclaims "*Jubilee!*" and we proclaim..."*Whew, that's me!*", but I look and see confession making people around me who claim to be blessed and highly favored. They are savoring the moment of a spiritual high to get us by during the week, but what we really seek is not God...but His promises. The church used to be a place of worshipping God but now it seems to be a den of people praying to purchase a hot rod...and God is not pleased. Our priorities are out of place, probably like a transgressor feels when he or she visits our places of worship and sees $500 suits on our backs yet no sense of compassion for him or her. Alter calls are no longer for those who are lost. It seems that now they are for those who need money piles to make them a *better* Christian. I believe in Jubilee, prosperity and the wealth transferring from the wicked to the just...but not from the wicked to the *just barely serving God*. We are subconsciously trying to *pimp* the Creator...claiming to be "prophets" when we are really only trying to *profit* off of an anointing that probably never came from God in the first place. Hypothetically speaking, it is first base, second, third, home...but our order is warped. It is causing our so-called spiritual discernment to give us hallucinations about streets of gold on Earth when the same streets are filled with lost people who hurt. The dirt is slowing covering the coffins of folk who are doomed for Hell's flames and yet we proclaim "Give me a blessing God!" instead of "Heal the lost." And I run to the altar and ask God to forgive me...for not having my spiritual priorities straight. I want to *be* a blessing and not always waiting with open hands ready to receive one. And I heed one warning...their blood will be on my hands. Forgive us God.

Things

Everybody wants *things*. We work to afford *things*.

We will lie, cheat, and steal for *things*.

And usually those *things* give birth to no*thing*.

Things.

Things will pull us by strings. A man will miss out on his good thing because she didn't meet every*thing* on his list of qualities.

Men will downgrade loving a woman simply to get that *thing*.

Women will upgrade a fling to love status because their heart is missing *things*.

Things.

But it's funny, we are quick to say, "It aint no *thing*."

When in fact it's every*thing*...

Things.

Things bring joy, hurt, sadness, laughter, grief, beautiful beginnings with suffering filled endings...sending people in a state of depression and to lessen the pain we obtain more...*things*.

Things.

It's interesting that in the Bible, the revival always come after all these *things* have come to pass.

"And it came to pass after these ***things***..."

"And it came to pass after these ***things***..."

Mentioned 24 different times in the Bible...

Results rival *things*.

Things...

Seems so general, seems so minimal, but our entire life revolve around *things*.

Our children want *things*. Our mates want *things*. Our jobs expect certain *things* out of us in order to pay us so we can pay for our *things*.

Things.

I wonder what would happen if we stopped focusing so much on *things?*

Granted some *things* we have to focus on...*Things* like bills, *things* like money, *things* like family, *things* like our health, *things* like our relationships with mates, family, co-workers, with God.

I mean He did say He would do a new *thing* in us...which can be translated as "I will make you fresh."

We are constantly praying for God to change us, when He actually needs to re-name us, reframe us, refrain us from trying to put something stale up for spiritual retail...trying to cut deals with God with a 50% off righteousness sale. Pull me out of this old shell. Make my Abram-Abraham, my Jacob- Israel, and my Saul- Paul, My Simon- Peter...We need a...rediscovery. For it is only then that God can uncover the new *thing* that He has done.

Things...

Seek ye first the Kingdom of God and His righteousness, and then all these *things* shall be added unto thee.

Things don't get you to the Kingdom...

Righteousness gets you those *things*...

The right *things*...

What is your *thing*?

In Everything Let Me See You

Once again I sit here ashamed and broken in spirit because I have given my all to someone or something else other than You. All too often the pattern of reverence and due honor is misconstrued in my heart knowing that You make all things possible in my life. Yet, I still, at times, express my love and adoration for another and subconsciously forget that it was You lovingly spake life into my body.

Father forgive me for placing you out of order in my spiritual flow chart of honor. There are so many elements in life that I daily mistake as a "given". Breath, air, freedom, nature, life itself, and continual grace on days that are not even promised are the things I feel as though will always be there at my disposal.

Throughout my whole life I have repeatedly heard the story of the saga at Calvary. The nails...the cross...the Blood...the sacrifice...the love for me.

Still, whole days slip by me, consumed by my daily agendas, and I forget the sacrifice of a Son You gave me over 2000 years ago. At that moment in my heart I attempt to fathom the idea of Your continual love and blessings on my life's endeavors, regardless of my subconscious ingratitude. There are those unexpected blessings that show up in the midst of my forgetting that You are there with me and it is Your strength that gets me through. The infinite love You give me...how can I forget? Your innumerable forgiving mercies...how could I forget? Your Hand of blessing constantly hovering over me...how can I forget? Your endless grace...how could I forget? Father I want to love You more and more each and every moment in my life.

Reveal Yourself afresh unto me moment by moment so that I may make You the center of attraction throughout the day. Remind me through people, places, and things that You live and move in all of life's endeavors.

Grant me the ability to see You through the trees, for they always honor Your greatness with uplifted branches and limbs in awe of Your Power. I hear birds chirping glorious melodies every break of morning in reverence of Your Spirit. Keep my spirit informed that You are ever present in my life, through every element that encamps about me daily. In everything let me see You. Never do I want to freeload off of Your grace and mercy. Every new day there is the first priority of kneeling down in submission to Your Power, praying that my steps are ordained for that days journey. No decisions will be made in haste, only guided my Your impeccable Wisdom. In everything, everyone and every element of my day; let me see You.

For Her

She was sleep when I called her...Tried to stall her so she
could to talk to me but she wouldn't.

She couldn't.

She was tired.

Didn't even say she loved me before hanging up.

I was hurt.

Been trying to wine her and dine her and remind her how
we were back in the day but it didn't work.

She was sprung out...Hard.

I wasn't man enough for her anymore.

She liked it rough now.

Liked the breaks beat off of it...and she loved it.

She wanted the thug type.

Had a thing for the grilled out niggas who had more love for
triggers than they did her.

She was merely...a piece.

See...she got molested a few years back and now she
misconstrues that for affection...

Erections only felt... but not seen because she is always
facing the wall with her thong string pulled to the

side...where niggas can slide in and out without ever acknowledging the beauty of her face...She has no trace of...her worth.

And she continues to give birth...to bastards.

Bastards who know not their father...because he is too busy making his rounds.

And I still want to be there...but she will not let me...

She thinks I am...a punk of sorts.

A punk who sports love around his neck as opposed to a chain...

A punk who actually uses his brain before lovemaking...taking his time to caress a rhyme...but she only likes being temporarily "hooked."

Word has it that she got infected with an S.T.D.

Stereotypical Thug Dialect...

So now I have to protect myself before touching her.

But she won't let me.

I miss the days where we could make love for hours in showers of melodies, harmonies and words that provoke change and revolution...but the confusion has her thinking that the best aphrodisiac is a snap and a clap...with braggadocio about being trapped in the trap...while being whispered to about waiting to see some twins' "d*&k..."

And I am quick...to write to and for her but I am ignored because I don't bust glocks, and sell rocks and would rather chop samples than ounces.

She bounces from bed to bed giving head...while the money is left on the nightstand without her hand ever being held in admiration of her virtue.

Tried to tell her that needs to cut back on the "beef"...it's making her sluggish and out of shape.

She is being raped.

Being videotaped for the whole world to see on BET...who is supposed to cherish her and represent her in the most positive light...but they like...to hit it too.

They like...to hit it too.

They like...to hit it too.

Wait...

Isn't that incest in a sense?

She has lost her innocence.

She is no longer recognizablc by the purists.

Her vagina now giving birth to somewhat autistic offspring who sing senseless gibberish about licorice sticks and "laffy taffy."

But "she likes it."

Her skirt...she hikes it...up high so this guy and that guy can run trains while simultaneously polishing the wood grain of their Phantom, and I just choose not to partake.

Would rather wait... until she comes to her senses.

I refuse to disrespect her and neglect her or subject her to some "5 minute" production process just to undress her.

I want to bless her...with life so we can give birth to a revolution and not pollution of the mind.

I think deep down inside she misses the royal treatment.

The way Donny used to treat her and the way Marvin used to romance her...and the way Luther used to dance with her...as if she was...his father.

So every night...I will continue to call her...hoping we can talk again...

Be friends again...

Blend again...

Be her penicillin so I can clear up the infection that was left from the young whippersnappers and the "whisperers and snappers", the cats that would whip her and slap her...for fame and a name...and defame her.

Something about her skin "tone".

When the wind is blown...I still hear Stevie's ribbon in the sky and think about her.

Now she only moves when the bass drum kicks with a depth of 808 and the stripper pole is oiled and ready for sliding...or the makeshift gangster is riding with his crew igniting a colliding with a rival gang who bangs for the sake of drug terrain...or the soundtrack to a "Prelude To A Slang" type episode where off white hallucinogens are sold to a black soul...for profit.

And they won't stop it.

And they won't stop it.

And these "lil" negores will not stop it.

But I will try...for her.

I will cry for her...I will deny self and sleep...for her.

I will die for her.

That's what love do.

Her name is Black Music.

A Letter To My Slave Mother

I hate what they did to you. If I could change history, I would. I could get mad at them, revolt and provoke them to war, but I am too busy warring with my own people...your own people. The same ones you died for are denied more freedom because we enslave each other now.

They call it black on black crime...having me, at times, afraid to walk in my own community, with the thought of being struck by visually impaired bullets.

The trigger...they pull it. Not conscious to the fact they are killing each other quite like the slave-owners did when they threw you overboard on the ships.

The clips are inserted...worded quite well by gangster rappers/gunslappers, and our sons have to walk home from school on these same wastelands...which gives the Klan the right to suggest, to each other, early retirement.

I heard they used to pack you on the bottom of the ships with chains. That is odd. The ghetto is just the same, but with a different name. It is a shame.

So-called musicians are exploiting you on our CD's and cassette decks' I guess, as the slave-owners would take you by the neck and beat you and rape. Make you do all types of hideous things for his lustful enjoyment.

Your body, he was exploring it...for his own gratification and musically the hip-hop nation is doing the same thing.

Same swing...different park...

Dark nights alone I sit and read history on how they did you and I won't kid you, I think I would have probably killed myself to.

This is a letter to you, slave mother, from a young brother who sees straight through the platinum and ice and sees the trap.

Yet they rap, and rap, and rap, and wrap themselves up in their own coffin, not knowing that a generation is dying slowly.

Slave mother; please show me the things you used to see. The pain you used to feel...the prayers you used to pray, the freedom songs that you would sing even in the midst of you being labeled less than a queen. The scene is hurting the eyes of my optimism. I need your wisdom to teach my sons how to respect you, and not to neglect you. And I regret you ever went through the horrors of the Middle Passage, but I ask this of you...teach me how to respect...your children.

My brothers...

My sisters...

A Matter of Trust

With righteousness I have cut covenant. The covenant cut back some cutthroats.

The cutthroats cut me back because righteousness and I became intimately involved.

I have evolved into a man who is few of friends who posed as such, much of which I am to blame...making decisions based on the exterior rather than the interior...superiority complexes hexed my pre-spiritual discernment.

It is a matter of trust.

I choose to lead the majority of my black life alone...Not entangling many into my "circle".

Judas'...they come a dime a dozen. People want to ride on the bandwagon of the anointed...but never appointed by God to speak life into me.

Modern day "prophets" who only "prophelie" to those who look as if they can enrich one's superficial hunt for the self-defined favor of God.

Fallacies spite my verses.... I see past the illusion. Causing confusion...

I am choosing the straight and narrow as I dine with sparrows...because at least I know that God's eye is never far from them.

Lies are cloned. Duplicated...replicated...laminated even to protect the nakedness of fibs.

My knees assume their usual nightly position...praying that hissing of deceitful snakes in my garden will be decoded and dissected and sent to the mainframe of the mechanism in my spirit that produces flawless discernment...and that I turn quick from those enemies who pose as my friends.

It is a matter of trust.

I shall stay alert to the slick tongued, man made verses of false prophets who only exhort to reap a harvest from a garden that has their same snake markings in them...or trees for that matter.

Matthew 7:15-23, Christ warned me about suspect prophets; wolves dressed up like sheep...thus I pray that God show me the "true" them by the fruit that they reap.

I must keep them at arms distance with a resistance against this witchcraft. Which math do we NOT understand? Bad fruit equals bad tree and bad tree equals bad seed...and I need to know them by their spirit...First.

I thirst discernment.

It is nothing personal.

It is just a matter of trust.

Common Ground (For Mr.)

I was awakened to the sound of my own weeping...seeking answers from a dream all too real.

With zeal, I tried to mentally bury you...figured I would worry you if I attempted reaching out to you. Doubt that you would reconsider the friendship that slipped on some many occasions...Abrasions to my soul are left untreated.

My mind's "hellos" to you left un-greeted...My fantasy of us actually working out...deleted.

Until I walked up to the casket and saw an older version of me laying their lifeless...it was you though...Life just...*well you know*...passes us by when bitterness withers less and less and begins to fester. The devil played the jester in my dreams but nothing was funny. I cried over a father that doesn't bother to act as if his love for me is valid...I wrote a ballad for us in my dreams..."*and when this life is over...remember when we were not together...I was alone and I was dreaming this dream of you...*"

Possibly it was God telling me to find you before the dream was a real life theme and I am standing over your casket crying over a father whose family didn't even bother to list me as a son on his obituary...possibly because I am looked at as a mistake. As I break...to weep again...trying to keep a friend who should be a friend by default considering he was responsible for littering in my mother's womb 33 years ago, and his trash became the treasure of a son...Me.

And to think...I really thought I had let this go...

And to think I really thought you would let me know...that you were still in existence at least.

If you die...not knowing whether or not I would cry, or even try...to come to your funeral is not good for me...Thus I will be...attempting again...to find you.

The search for you...

The search for me...

The search for we.

Common ground.

Collective Judgment

The light reflected off the dome of the Grand Palace as the iniquities of the people were suddenly exposed. They held their heads in shame as, by name, their sins were called off one by one according to each individual's purpose. It seemed worthless at this point, the shining glitter of their watches and rings, blings and shoestrings attached to their Air Forces as remorse filled the atmosphere as fear latched onto their hearts.

It was the collective judgment.

The music came to a screeching halt as they screamed, "It wasn't my fault", as the failures of their seeds were called out in rapid succession.

In the background was the black sound of crying from innocent boys and girls who were hurled into a world of fiending for themselves as the shelves of library books were filled to capacity; asking the question, "Who am I?", a worth never validated by momma and daddy.

The seeds began to interrogate the parents as directed by the Almighty One who could not reverse the curse of ignorance because He would have to renig on His Written Word. One lad asked his dad was his car more important than the assortment of thoughts he had about his level of learning whom teachers said was remedial, yet daddy's residual support for school work was minimal. His father couldn't answer. The cancer of dumbfoundedness began to eat away at daddy's bones as his son's moans became louder with each second of fatherly silence, "You don't love me do you?"

Father cried as he saw a glimpse of the future for his son which was filled with guns and desire to do whatever it took to make a couple of ones...and collecting funds for bail.

Jail.

Locked up for never being loved by father...

Sentence?

Birth to death...no possibility of parole...

There was this beautiful young girl...not fully developed mentally, but physically had the measurements of a full grown woman.

Her mother, much like her, confused sex for acceptance and begin birthing seeds in her early teens...screams of "Love me please!!!", sounded much like, "I'll get down on my knees....to beg!!"

Two raised and parted legs...fertilized eggs.

The mother wept as she kept seeing the same curse rehearsed...birth after birth after birth. No self worth instilled in the mind of her daughter as her water broke repetitiously for years and years. The tears streamed as she screamed, "Baby girl, don't be like me!!" But despite the cries and the water in her eyes, baby girl kept getting hexed by the lies, and her thighs her always getting rubbed by strange men who changed when the EPT show plus signs.

It was a collective judgment.

"Train up a child in the way he should go and when he is old he will not depart from it"; is what the Almighty kept repeating, but they kept deleting this line from their life's script.

It was a trip down the future's lane as the parents became more aware that life is to lived for seeds and not selfish needs...or wants. One flaunts the designer shoes and automobiles, and spinning wheels and skirts but hurts the child who was never assured that he or she was loved. Boys left to be validated by the block, and glocks. Girls mocked by hard rocks who watch for signs of weakness...because a mother was speechless when baby girl asked, "Am I a jewel?"

You'll be left to watch this cycle be recycled until the revival of self worth is taught in your seed's curriculum of life.

Knife to the routine of the fallacies of keeping it real and instilling the lie that love is for the weak; men.

Knife the routine that you gotta do what you gotta to get what you want even if it means to flaunt your goods; women.

Can't you see the signs? I want to see the blinds opened from our minds and refine the times when self worth was top priority and when men took the authority in the homes. The clones of penitentiary heroes are giving our young ones zeroes in life's scorebook of manhood.

I demand the good to be refurbished and refined because a nine seems to say, I love you better than a hug do.

We have lost focus, I repeat, we have lost focus and quote this to all that are guilty.

The blood of the seed rests on the bearer of them.

Love them.

It was a collective judgment.

Don't be found guilty.

Willie Lynch (Will He Lynch?)

I am Willie Lynch. I am the stench in young negroes nose that grows more and more unbearable with every parable about real *niggerdom*. Niggers come to my mental meetings as I am seating them beside their enemies...winning me more and more votes through every "kill a nigga" quote. With every "tote a nine" rhyme I design death around a dollar sign and intertwine the lime light, but it don't shine bright...long. Your child's favorite is a drug kingpin and serial killer, a material dealer of "scrilla" laced hate. See that is my bait. I call it *trapped in the trap* rap. They adapt clap to gun claps. Maps of gang territory are used to tell of story with gory details of black males and gun shells dropping, never stopping to think. They shrink the trees I used to hang you on down to notebook paper to write rhythmic eulogies.

Bloody rhymes I emit 'til Emmitt Till is relived over and over with black hands as the guilty party. I am hardly noticed...see I dress in the latest fashions...cashing in off of your ignorance. I made bulletproof vests trendy and come in different designs, see I deal solely with the mind. I made hip hop mostly a school for the blind.

Just credit Willie for street credibility. See they don't credit ability. They credit a bill; you see it's all about the benjamins. See I *been jamming* since I introduced my plan to mentally destroy the black man by simply putting a mic in his hand.

Will He lynch?

I am the Grinch that stole the soul out of black music. I made gunshots like hi hats, and hands that used to clap are hands that now sell crack to you blacks who use facts about how bad the ghetto is an excuse to poison kids lyrically. Kids who cannot distinguish the difference between nonfiction and a video vixen... Kids get silly when exposed to folding of monetary paper in high volume. I have collapsed the columns that held up the covering of black togetherness.

I can now make them rap about anything. Female lyricists will descriptively crown their beautiful birth canals as the kryptonite to the big ballers, who in turn will be the subject of baby daddy narratives who are paying for blinged out baby carriages.

Strong black kings will demand that their gangsta be respected and their pimp tendencies to be idolized by idol eyes who sees nothing but a father figure in it smallest context. My *con* is the *text* for destroying a strong black culture.

I am the most successful pimp in the business...and my hoes are those that have chose to pose as those who wear white robes with pointed hoods with eye holes, doing gangsta rap ciphers around burning crosses propped in potholes, and as the plot grows thicker, the quicker they succumb to me.

Will he lynch??

But the fact remains; I hate anything remotely resembling the unification of black people. A deep rooted hate that has caused me to device a plan so grand that they think I am actually *for* them. I ignore them in my thoughts of longevity though, see I kill very slow.

Just think for a minute. They are the only race that glorifies genocide. They have renamed their rides *whips*. With their lips they defend me in interviews saying that I am "only entertainment." They subconsciously pay homage to me. But I am the *Big Willie*. They are so silly.

They don't think about the fact that alternative rockers don't refer to themselves as glock cockers and block lockers, and stockers of cocaine to sell to their own people's brains.

They look beyond the fact that when Marvin used to sing, and James Brown would bring the funk, Negroes came together to question authority and raise the minority mind state. Now they align cake with success and never bless their sons. I got them rapping at adolescent ages now. Kids who are barely able to carry the weight of the mic can recite about carrying weight. Marrying hate and divorcing the innocence of youth to be young G's. I have made them deem hotrods as their God and gang terrain will train young minds to kill over land that they do not even own, and Patron has become their holy water. They border on extinction because of the lack of knowledge.

I am so pleased with my accomplishments.

I will single handedly destroy the black mind through warped expressions of art. I will single handedly destroy the black mind through warped expressions of art. I will single handedly destroy the black mind through warped expression of art.

So the next time you hear a rhyme designed around a nine in a fist's clinch...ask yourself...will he lynch?

Never

There is nothing about you that I would overlook...even down to the simplest detail of the way your cold in your eyes is shaped in our mid morning conversations.

Everything about you screams divine...seems designs of you were strategic before time was shaped.

Bait of my soul's hook, but nothing fishy about you...you overwhelmed my spirit's lake.

If I hieroglyphically fluent I would draw pictures of you inside ghetto pyramids fully clothed with a naked soul so my brothers could see the depth of your original mold.

Blame it on my mother, I just can't help but to worship your strength...the way you intuitively breach dishonest contracts before I immaturely sign our lives away...my today is only a tomorrow waiting to relive our yesterday again.

Never understood why now you downsized to a thong and hip-hop hook, when it's seems only yesterday you were the subject of Donny Hathaway's sadness when you left him, and how he wept for your return.

Let me learn of thee, my sister...a wisdom like that of Nikki and Sonia...spiritually swapping the Songs of Solomon through semi-second eye glances.

I am not afraid to tell you that without you I was without me.

I am not afraid to tell you that without you I was without me.

I am not afraid to tell you that without you I was without me.

Without a she a he is not a complete me.

And I don't see how they don't understand this...how they just reprimand this, "Cherish our women" proclamation.

I am hating in its most complex form.

I will be called a bitch for you.

I will be called soft for you.

I will be honored to wear the badge of punk nigga for the sake of your integrity.

It is all because of my love for you.

My love for the look in your eyes when you tell me about myself...

The look of "I don't care what you got as long as I got you", when I fantasize about sharing a non-existent wealth.

The excitement I get when I hear your heels strike the floor when you are entering the door after I haven't seen you all day. The way you recite old school rhymes word for word with me while listening to old school tapes.

This is why I will never disrespect you.

I will never degrade or exploit you.

I will never call you out of your name.

I will never stop loving you.

Never.

I promise.

Beautiful Eyes

I know it probably torments you day to day. The way you laid up on that table and made a decision in haste...The waste of a missed menstrual sucked through the clinic tubes.

But I still love you...whoever you are.

A star is...not born...Left to mourn...playing funeral songs in your mind from the sight of a casket that was never opened.

A child with an unrecognizable face...one you never beheld.

But mentally you can't leave this imaginary area...Scarier than "monster in the closet" thoughts as a child...but...Smile again...you are forgiven.

Beautiful eyes.

I hear your cries...as you mentally wipe what was supposed to be your baby's eyes; as you despise the would-be father who said, "I ain't ready for no baby!"...The same rabid dog that would spread your legs and beg you to believe that his love for you was undefiled and pure. But sure enough...the bluff was unmasked when you asked, "Have you been sleeping a lot lately?"

I have issues with a man who can quickly come up with abortion funds, yet tell his woman "no" when she asks for a couple of ones...just to come and see him.

The grim reality?

You were supposed to have kids...with those cute little Osh Kosh lids and baby bibs...who dibs and dabs in everything...and wants to ride on every swing in every park...and it's very dark when you are alone with those denied embryo nightmares...but...right there is where I want to be telling you that you are forgiven.

Beautiful eyes.

Pro-life advocates deny you the right to be pardoned by the Almighty, when nightly men send their women on guilt trips with lips that deny fatherhood. It is so strange to me how a man can deny what he knows to be his baby...but up until the moment of truth he never had trust issues with his lady. Maybe I am a little extreme but it seems that as a "God fearing" society we tend to ignore the 3 am screams of women who didn't do it just to stay on the club scene...but with dreams of a fatherless seed who needs love and support and not just occasional child support. The remedy, to abort. Thoughts of spending half the day in court...Maybe some want to produce children whose father frequently snorts...poison. The voice in your head torments like... "You should have had him" or "By now he would be two" or "How can you kill you mother's grandbaby?"...As the lady sings the blues in your spirit.

A friend's newborn...you can't go near it...because your deceased seeds cries; you are scared you will hear it.... And the breakdown and exposure of what you hid in the closet for years...you fear it.

Led to think that you are this evil specimen of a woman with a contaminated integrity... Begging the visions to go away as you pray "God...please take this guilt away"...feeling like a pound of filth is added to your withering womanhood per day. I pray that you realize you are forgiven and that God loves you and that you still have...

Beautiful eyes.

Beautiful eyes that will, in Heaven, behold the child whom you had to forsake.

Eyes that will see the child hug you and say..."Mommy I have been waiting on you", as if you never made a mistake. And I take time out of my normal poetic agenda full of social commentary and racial issues to give sonnet like tissues to every beautiful woman that has given up the seeds...I need you to know that...you are forgiven.

We are all living on borrowed time...and in mind sometimes I wish my own mother would have gone done the procedure but God needs a man that is compassionate enough to say that He loves you in spite of your mistake. You are so beautiful...and even though it may not have been worth it, nobody is perfect.

I wish I could wipe your eyes and hold you through your midnight cries.

They are lies...the ones who tell you that God hates you...no God makes you...a new, forgiven woman...daily. God is love.

They say you can cut a Lamb's throat and it will lick your hand while it dies.

That Lamb is Jesus Christ...and it for all of our sins and mistakes for which died.

You are forgiven...pretty girl...with your *beautiful eyes*. I love you.

Battered

Why do you have those black rings around those beautiful eyes; contacts the color of hurt? Did he hit you again? Did he pretend that he loved you, beat you and then hug you and reward himself with your body for apologizing to you before bruises turned a hateful shade of blue? Is this how he portrays love to you? Does he make you his self-appointed Salem witch? Does he make you his bitch...female dog...hump you indiscreetly like a stray Pitbull...infecting you with domestic abuse rabies...giving you babies that fear him just as you? You hate that you love him and love that you hate him and subconsciously you want guys in prison to rape him and make him what he made you...a body void a soul. He made your bedroom a jail cell and forced his rage on your femininity and you wonder why the pro-choice crowd hates you because your pregnancies don't add up to your births, but it's not worth the pain. You reside with a direct descendent of satan himself but presently he is your only source of financial health, and your self esteem is only found when your face is down and your body is...his pleasure zone. He sits on his throne and you sit alone...telling the kids that he hits you because he loves you and they see hate as love and instantly and innocently they wonder why love leaves scars...on the exterior. The mirror shows you the outer evidence of a bad decision to take him up on his offer to take you out on a date years back and your tears smack your cheek, and you are too meek, too weak to fight him off...and the cycle begins again.

Anger...Not your fault...physical assault...next comes sex.

Anger...Not your fault...physical assault...next comes sex.

Anger...Not your fault...physical assault...next comes sex.

Anger...Not your fault...physical assault...next comes sex.

Positive pregnancy test...satan at his best or worst, cursed the womb with a preconceived demonic seed.

Lack of love produces bastards who beat their girlfriends, and rape their own wives. Men who mistake their woman's child harboring stomach for kick-balls and they hit walls and spit balls of insidious remarks to spark a dead flame...with the name "*HURT MALE*" invisibly stamped on their hearts.

The cycle will not end.

He is not your friend.

He hates you. He dictates you. He makes you...his source of lost love.

Are You Sure?

Sister, are you sure because it ain't no cure? Are you sure because it ain't no cure?

They say about one of every 10 men got a "friend "that they girl thinks "Oh, they just being men". That "he like my brother significant other", they dog, they homie, they "bone me" when ain't nobody looking partner.

Pardon the French, but "we-we" got Kee-Kee taking the "keep me alive another year" medication cause "you better call Tyrone" took on a whole new meaning.

Sisters are dreaming of knight in shining armor and not a night of latex and safe sex. It placed all bets off. "Cough, cough" that's the same cold you had 6 months ago?

Rugged hands, mechanical man...Sisters all hype because they got the thug type ...but they didn't know he wasn't referring to cars when he talked about "tailpipes."

My queens are looking for the twang' in the voice and the bent wrist; that's too obvious. Solving this dilemma is a must. The trust has been crushed.

Too many are ending up with that Terry McMillan feeling. Dealing their life out on the table like a bad hand of poker because sister lets him poke her... without strapping up...without backing up before boxers drop and stop to analyze the guys he hang with, slang with, "do the thang" with...while he Ying Yang with his boy.

"Twon" don't want you..."Twon" got yo' Fonz who thinks he is 100% hetero' because he never blows...he never gets low...he never gets severed below the waist...He only gives and then allows you to take home...the evidence.

Cats with tattooed backs and slacks residing below cracks, pushing Cadillacs with "thug nasty" on they front plates be some of the same ones whose train is ran into they "man."

Got me praying, "*Our Father which art in heaven...Thy Kingdom come but Thy kings have cum inside another man. Thy will be done, but your son is sexing your other son and still claiming sanity.*" Give us this day our daily, "Maybe I need to reevaluate my life" type thought and not get caught up in the lies....but thighs are still opened and sisters are still hoping for a cure because they were sure he wasn't like that and let him go bareback.

Where do we lack proper judgement?

My sister; are you sure?

It ain't no cure.

Every Season

Using any theorem, my love for you squared is the equivalent of infinite degrees of earthly manifestations of Heaven. If seven is the Biblical symbolism of completion...then you are the one to my six, the three to my four, the five to my two, the end to my pain, the new to my beginning...the ending to my search for a soul mate.

If I had every nation's armed forces lined up to battle me, and I was granted one wish, it would that you be the captain to my, now, two man army, and simply arm me with your intuition.

Your mind is revered by my soul.

When night comes, I envision you and I parallel like spoons underneath sheets made of Egyptian cotton, nestled close with thoughts of sweet conversation right at room temperature. See, your interpretation of destiny filled dreams warm me in the morning.

In perfect synchronization, I dance with angels mentally at midday when I think of how blessed I am to call you "ma'am" when sit me down to tell me the errors in my hasty decision making...all while creating strategic plans to right them.

You have humbled me enough to somehow *enjoy* being corrected, knowing that lesson learned will be one passed to generations of scholars bearing our namesake.

On hot summer days you are more than my spirit's cool breeze, you are the more like the unseasonably low 64 degree, 5 straight days of relief from the sweltering humidity.

I have yet to fully comprehend that slight grin during our moments of silence. It's almost like a subliminal conformation of the consummation of our dreams and goals that will give birth to the solutions of the world's problems as a whole. You have a way of words without speaking, a way of enlightening me without teaching...a way of prophesying to my bones without preaching prolific sermons of that of a seasoned biblical scholar sporting a collar ...representing his depth of knowledge concerning religious structure.

As I muster up ways to describe your worth, I mentally find myself in what is seemingly a dry desert trying to convince the cactus that it, only a daily basis, experiences the pleasure of an innocent rain every morning dripping from it's thorns...all while it is dying.

And I am trying to prove to myself that this can happen to anybody...but it can't...

And I am trying to prove to myself that this can happen to anybody...but it can't...

And I am trying to prove to myself that this can happen to anybody...but it can't...

You were meant only for me...

So I will trying to understand it and just demand it never cease...

Meant to be...

Meant to be...

You were only meant for me...

You are my every season.

Unmask My Macho

I will unmask my macho for you.

I need to understand that every time you are crying I don't have to be inclined to design a resolution...as the solution is sometimes released during the conclusion of tears falling...and my job is solely to hold you and not try to mold you into something stronger.

At times, I have to step aside of my father's theories, get near thee and realize that I need to listen to you, shut my mouth, and dissect my baby's "Maybe this will work if..."

I verbally acknowledge your gift, but stray from the practice of my preaching, subliminally teaching my son that only daddy's wisdom holds weight.

A moment of clarity will hold open the gate. My macho needs to go far away on a blind date with reality and realize that a great majority of my destiny's casualties were from a lack of female intuition...Mental e-mails from you sent directly to deletion not realizing they were the completion of my plans...telling myself, "I am a man!"

Funny, I can profess my love to you all day yet rarely stay to hear you out...then when you shout, I say you have an attitude.

Your love whispers, your love screams, your love dreams of ways to make our lives easier collectively...but I am neglecting she who silently destroys the ceilings that I built that stop my own progress. However, I still will not confess that I am blessed...to have a woman with an honest opinion.

Sometimes machismo equates to your man being idiotic.

And my confession is a start...

And my confession is a start...

I'm sorry that, to you, I didn't listen and decode the hissing of snakes in my dream's garden and have to keep starting over and over when Plan A, B, and C fail...Then in turn I immaturely yell," You weren't there for me."

It is clear to me now that I married you to divorce selfish plans...sitting here with helpless hands...claiming I am tired when the help I hired at the alter is staring at me with only one demand, "Just listen to me baby."

Lady, without you, I am never accomplishing my goals fully. Thus, I need you. I understand now when you give me your opinion and advice it may not always be nice, but that's because you care for me.

And I am sorry.

Please, take off this mask for me...so I can see the gift that you are.

A Prayer on Behalf Of My Brothers

We need You. We have lost our direction and we have lost our discretion, and the question is...where are you GOD? It's hard being us...seeing trust evade us and it has made us vengeful and sinful and we are walking in this present day Garden of Eden...deceiving ourselves into thinking we are pimps and players when are actually the slayers of our own morality. We are blind to reality with this "carry me" syndrome. *Carry me* to the block and *carry me* to the weed spot and we heed not the warnings of our forefather's spirit saying, "Behave...you are still a slave." We are beating ourselves with liquor bottle bullwhips and diseased prostitute's lips, and our mind, body and soul chains now come masqueraded as crack cocaine and we have left our sisters at home laying...waiting for us to resurrect. We no longer cry...we kill. We feel that our masculinity is based on protecting our personal vicinity and anyone befriending us is the enemy...and it's sending me to my knees night after night.

We want the title "baby daddy" instead of "father" not knowing that it takes more than sending a check to raise a toddler. And some of us don't bother. We hurt our kids by only showing up when another man wants to take on the "daddy roll" because we crave control.

A great majority of us don't know why we are mad. We
don't know why we beat our wives. We don't know
ourselves; yet on our shelves...sits the Bible...dusty and
forsaken.

God...you have experienced our pain. Your Son went
through just the same. Rejected and neglected...No honor
in his own hometown/ ghetto/suburban dwelling and they
are telling us subliminally that we are still only worth 3/5.
All of us don't have gifts. All we have is what we have...a
name on the waiting list of pessimistic statistics. Martins'
and Malcolms' and Marcus' and Fredricks' come one in a
million, yet there is a one in fifteen chance that I will be the
victim of a black killing...and it's chilling. That is why some
of us are so on edge. Some of us feel like we are constantly
walking on a ledge and walking on the shells of eggs,
nervous and frustrated with social cramps in our legs.

Our own sisters think we are too light or too dark, or not
enough education...with high expectations and low patience
and our relations are dysfunctional. *This function will* cease
if we learn to release our cares on You.

Our fathers were drunks and their fathers were abusers
thus we don't know why we consistently drink and violently
vent our anger and endanger the lives of those closest to us.
We are broken hearted and confused...socially, mentally
and financially abused, and the choices we choose are
limited to our mind's capacity.

Tragically we are dying and our women and children are crying and trying to understand why daddy is gone. Our friends surround us but we still feel alone. We feed on this bone that is handed to us because we are treated as "dogs". We cannot see through this fog...clouding our minds as we look through these blinds and see project bricks in our mental. Corporate Grand Central stations are placing us on trains of thought that have us thinking we were created to be servants and slaves to CEO's, working two and three jobs cleaning boardrooms and bathrooms and then try to have room to spend time with our seeds? Our pleas are not heard because it is hard to be audible while at the bottom of the totem pole you are dwelling.

We resort to drug selling and lie telling to get ahead and our blood is shed; yet it speaks from the ground like Abel when we are dead...and our seeds are misled.

We are lied on...misunderstood...hunted like prey exuding the scent of blood for our black potency...and we are quoting the verses of rappers rather than God's word and then we wonder why we are not heard. We wonder why we are taken for a joke.

We wonder why we are sporting the latest fashions and still broke. We still choke...because these hereditary nooses are robbing us of our true identity...and our father's demons are sending us to places we really don't want to go; but we are like a kid in a candy store...we can't resist. We can't kiss our sons, but we can beat them and mistreat them. We need them to understand that the words; "I love you" was never uttered from granddaddy's lips...just how to properly grab a woman's hips. We want to cry but we are scared that we won't stop and we can't drop our pride and release all the pain and the demons from the inside. We tried to love our women...but our daddies told us it was more important to show her who has the upper-hand and who wears the pants rather than dance and romance our wives. Our lives...on trial... guilty by racial default...assault charges. Leaving us caught. Caught between bad choices and choices we didn't make...like our gender and race, and we face death in so many various facets...leaving us lost and bewildered. We are deceived and disoriented making us more resented by those who cannot fathom the struggle we go through.

God I would show You...but I know You already see that most of us don't want to be: hustlers and thugs, addicted to drugs and allergic to hugs and ones who mug...disloyal to our sisters, and "dead beat daddys" and pushing pimp like Caddy's, and woman abusers and losers. But some of us don't see...we are confined to a "Martin Luther King, Jr. Drive mentality." Open our eyes to reality. Let us have unclogged pipe dreams of once again being kings.

We are calling out to You through our folly...Calling out to You through our mischief and mistakes. We are calling out to You yet falling through...cracks and crevices. Never this much pain did we imagine. Since slavery we have been internally hurting. We deal with it through flirting with death and disregarding our health. We are bound by self-hatred because our fathers called us punks and beat us. And their daddy beat. And their daddy beat them. And their daddy beat them. This genetic stem of hate, womanizing, alcoholism are blooming on these vines of demonic forces and the source of healing lies in You oh God.

We are slowly becoming number one on the list of race and gender suicides because we can no longer hide from this stress and pain. We don't even know our names...and in our brains is distortion and contortion and simultaneous remorse in our mind when are doing crime and while doing time...we wonder why we do the things we do and consistently stray away from You...and deep down inside we are screaming...GOD WE NEED YOU!

Give us back our identity please...God.

A Curb and a Dance

His name was Derrion Albert...16 years old...honor student.

Beaten to death...

Not shot, not stabbed...

Beaten...to death...without a wooden railroad tie, left on the side of a curb to die...while the camera rolled I heard a young girl cry, "They killing him, they killing him, Oh my God!!!!"

Online execution...all because he was trying in de-fusing the brawl...

Beaten to death...head crushed by a wooden pole...brain swollen inside his cranium, draining him of his life...and he died...on the curb.

It was midday...Chi-town...death on the curb.

The sun was shining...death on the curb.

Cars drove by...death on the curb.

Onlookers simply watched...a death...on...the curb.

Future scholar...dead on the curb.

I cried while watching the footage...Hate I ever clicked the link...I flinch to think that some our youth are 100% desensitized to preserving the lives of their brothers...As mothers weep.

Death sleeps...on the curb...

It seems we have become our own KKK and Neo-Nazi, "Watch me kill this nigga" minus the hoods, swastikas and, burning crosses and our young black men are earning losses...while yearning for applauses for how gangsta of a nigga they are...Achieving a star on the Thug Walk of Fame.

A shame it was so savage...so savage to watch they had to blot out the final scene of his last dream of hoping to catch his breathe....and then he died...on the curb.

But she lived through hers.

The unnamed 15 year old girl...raped...for 2 and a half hours.

Right outside of a school dance...raped for 2 and a half hours.

Her womanhood barely developed...raped for 2 and half hours.

Various forced entrances...for 2 and half hours.

Onlookers watched and cheered even... for 2 and half hours.

Some joined in.... for 2 and half hours.

What was going through her mind...for 2 and half hours?

What poison was infiltrating her blood stream...for 2 and half hours?

Multiple minute men took their turns trespassing and littering in her womb....for two and a half hours.

Raping her, degrading her, defacing her temple...for two and half hours.

And every day for the rest of her life...she will probably think about this every 2 and a half hours....

I remember the very day my niece was born 15 years ago...when I held her in my arms, not wanting to let go.

I remember when I heard her call me Uncle for the first time...The line was such a sweet sound.

Now I am thinking, "My niece is a little lady now...

In high school now...Liking boys now..."

After hearing about this...I fear this could have been her...Wishing I could not leave her unprotected for more than 2 and half hours.

Hoping she isn't wrongfully deflowered.

And by these thoughts; my soul was devoured.

Some of us can't even get along with our mates for 2 and half hours.

Some of us for the whole year have not even read our Bibles for a whole 2 and half hours.

Our prayer life has not even equaled 2 and half hours.

We will not even spend quality time with our children for 2 and half hours.

But we will stay on Internet for more than 2 and half hours.

We will gossip for more than 2 and half hours.

I will watch a football for more than 2 and half hours.

I will go two and a half days and not even call to check on my mom.

Yet she suffered, cried, yelled, while these demonic bombs exploded inside her womb.

And a tomb would have probably been a better place than looking up at the face of men who took her soul from her body...for 2 and half hours.

Our children are hurting...on the inside...and one another.

And just to think...it could have only taken one conversation to change these men that lasted less than 2 and a half hours.

Just 2 and half hours...

Derrion lay on the curb dying...and she lay on her back crying...and I am trying to understand...where we...went wrong?

A Curb and a Dance

Confessions &

Ramblings

Us

I want to know what makes you; you. I want to know what makes me; me.

I wanna know what makes us, *us*.

Is it the trust?

Is it is love?

Is the lack thereof?

Is it, possibly, all of the above?

Is it the hug after an argument that makes it all better even when the situation is still unresolved? Knowing that it will rise with us tomorrow...

We are playing the blame game, when both of us have guilt residing within, riding the thin line of perceived innocence with every sentence justifying immature acts.

Like a stack of dirty laundry sprayed down with Febreze, hoping that it will cover the odor of the disease of self righteousness...not admitting when we are wrong...Prolonged nights without kisses is all it equates to...makes you think... "Is it really worth all this?"

Wanting a kiss...but you turn your head...leave the bed...left me for dead emotionally...supposedly we had agreed that no night would wake up with a "make up" that was supposed to happen before our eyes closed...but we chose to break our own rules.

Fools we have labeled ourselves.

Our shelves that once housed beautiful love letters and sweaters that we bought just because we thought the other would look good in it...have been stocked with cold shoulders and hot eyes, humble pies that were never baked, forgiveness raked underneath pride...trying to hide the fact that we are only human who sometimes falter in our thought patterns....and we are only battling ourselves.

See; when I'm mad at you, and you're mad at me...it's *us* that suffer the most.

The togetherness element of you and I will die if we don't try and come to a resolution...

Understand that I need you.

Understand that I bleed you when my soul is lacerated and that Cupid was masqueraded before I met you. At last he was unmasked and I realized that you were his sidekick...and inside me the seed of destiny kicks and I want you to be holding my hand when I give birth to our future.

It's not about you...It's not about me...It's about us.

It's not about you...It's not about me...Baby, it's about us.

If "U.S." was an acronym it would the gem of one word that would revolutionize love…

Unselfish.

Serpent and My Conscience on the Tree

Delicious fruit...sure looks appealing....I want to eat of it, inject this into my system like drugs... my Eve ain't even around this time, just me, a serpent, and my conscience on the tree.

Serpent says to me, "Go ahead and eat it dog, it ain't going to hurt nothing."

My conscience said, "You know you shouldn't". The two battle aggressively. It's stressing me. I continue to admire this sin scented, sun tinted delicacy.
Hmmmmmm...Confirm this is okay, please, as I in turn stray away from the bending of knees...I want to partake.

Serpent says, "You know you want to taste it."

Righteousness sounds like incessant babble.

I battle with the two.

Battle rages on.

And on...

And on...

And on...

Long and drawn out I decide to nibble and deal with the consequences later...Whether lesser or greater I become reprobate.

My mind stands void of judgment as my nibbles become bites, and my bites become "right"...and my rights are really wrongs masqueraded in infatuated lust. Must I sit back and ask for forgiveness once more when I saw the evil coming forth out its cocoon? Soon the reality evolves...I reap what I sow...I know the enemy has won again. Sin traps me daily...blossoming on this same tree only in different forms coming in women and money, bad choices and quick schemes of success. I digress...and realize I am a branch on the tree of knowledge of good and evil.

Adam stands as the acronym of all men...

All

Day

Attacked

Massively

I say sarcastically..."The devil made me do it."

True it may be...but I have a conscience that warns me of decisions that will infect my destiny...Let this be... a warning to all men...

God's grace will not always strive with man always...it pays
to think twice .

Serpent says, "I got you this time."

God says, "Though he made a mistake...He's still mine."

Thank you Father...for you grace and mercy. Amen.

Church Girl

Not only are you attractive, but your integrity meters are peaking at the highest levels. Your decibels of virtue are loud...yet clouds of mystery hover over you...frequently breaking to invite the sunrays of "I keeps it real" through. And you are so fine. Not blind, obviously, to the fact that single male eyes are righteous roaming for that "good thing" prize.

Wise and intelligent...I sneak audible peeks into your conversation.

Church girl.

Hair always fly...toes and nails tell of a slight salon chair obsession. Questions I ask myself when I see you, "What would it be like to be your possible mate? Are you the kind of woman I ask out on a date, or are you the "let's do lunch" type without the hype of labeling something "seeing each other?" My mother even asked about you...as it relates to me...as it relates to a possible future "us", thus I wonder how I can enhance your vision. Decision made, I shall approach you.

Church girl.

"What's your schedule like during the week? Possibly, we can have dinner." No need for introductions, I have known you through Sunday morning greetings...subconsciously hoping I can progress past calling you "Sister So and So" up to maybe "baby", or "boo". Whatever is holy, of course. Waiting for your answer, I try not to let my eyes stray to places they shouldn't, but you are looking so good...and pure...and holy...and honest...and just; thus I think on those things.

Suddenly I start to think rejection, but the suggestion is made, "What about Friday night?" Right at 8 we agree to meet. Discreet in my approach we meet at the restaurant with a holy hug that somewhat stirs my flesh. Possibly it was those curves in that dress or maybe too long of an embrace...a trace of curiosity enters my psyche.

"Let me get that chair for you." Cordials are exchanged. "You look so nice", as you reciprocate just the same. Entrees are explained and...cleavage overtakes my brain.

Church girl.

Conversations begin about various visions and current events with hints of theory thrown in. Grown and sophisticated adults vibing on the same level, but then the devil jumps in.

Dialogue went from family trees to college degrees, or lack thereof, to job classifications to reparations, to economics to religious folks to Bible Study notes, to Pastor's quotes, to Genesis through Revelations back to Psalms, Proverbs and

Song of Solomon and she asks with a slight grin, "How do you feel about massages?"

Seed planted.

Granted, I don't try to be all deep and spiritual but it would take a miracle for a brother not to think flesh after this feminine quest for an answer.

Suddenly the mood shifts...Can't think of a spiritual answer to a fleshly question, with the enemy suggesting, It's only a question", but here's a quick lesson.

Massaging equals touching and feeling, and touching and feeling leads to heightened desire followed by muscular relaxation, and muscular relaxation equals the fast multiplication of declining thoughts of abstaining, and the declining thoughts of abstaining equals a modern Samson in training and...I aint even answered the question yet.

"What kind? Shoulder and neck or full body?" Naughty me.
She winked.

Church girl.

"I used to give my mom shoulder massages." Trying to offset the threat of Marvin Gaye type healing...but I am feeling her so...right now.

Church girl.

It's funny; I never would have thought that she thought on the level. The Devil wins again. Warped perception, a deception of sorts...

I am beginning to see a different side. A side that hides in church...A side that hides in the barely below the knee skirts...a side that flirts with my "Loose That Man and Let Him Go" declaration. A side that thirsts to see how far I can be pushed, or pulled in that matter.

Church girl.

I am trying to maintain. I am trying to stay focused. I am trying to chill.

I am trying...to follow her home...but...she...is...driving...too...fast.

Church girl.

"Innocent visit" I tell myself. It's just an innocent visit. My inhibitions challenge the supposed verdict. Evidence states otherwise.

"Have a seat." She greets meet an extensive CD collection full of Luther, Marvin, Coltrane, and Miles. She smiles...popped in some Isley...sat down beside me, and then...she tried me.

"So...where's my massage?"

(continued on next page)

And the conviction was so strong...I couldn't even enjoy breakfast in bed.

Misled...by me.

Church girl.

The Dog Whisperer

Women have come and gone and I am left with empty condom packets while my heart mimics the scene.

Gimmicks and dreams I have lived out through poetry and song. Venomous licks and thongs have taken many chunks of manhood and fed them to me as my mother warns me of a scorned woman's wrath.

The math never added up though. One plus one equals not enough in my book sometimes, thus a find a third party and urge her body to merge with my naughty triangle of mangled emotions, and end up falling again. I am stacking fornication on top of dishonesty...sleeping with a woman who ain't my wife and another who ain't even my girl.

Three worlds colliding now, with two not knowing, one knowing too much, the two knowing something is up, but too deep in love to question the un-resting intuition that is fishing through their mind time after time.

I align my thoughts with that of a Solomon following, swallowing up women as unknowing polygamy victims...licked them of their doubts about my faithfulness

196

yet never marrying...leaving them carrying the seed of a prophetic heartbreak that my art makes seem so obsolete in their mind.

If all men are dogs then who are their masters? Every bastard has a wayward father who bothers their seed through warped inherited traits and makes us do things that terrorize us during periods of loneliness.

Seems our only escape from the mental rape is to drape our penis in latex and play "sex will make it better" games...leaving our dames without names until God proclaims "wife" to our spirit.

But God can't speak clean thoughts to a dirty receptacle, thus I remain skeptical about who is really "the one" until I deal with me.

I have seen many a divorce and many a source of encouragement after 30 years of happiness. I have seen many a womanizer and a despiser of their soul-mate. I have seen adultery served on a cold plate and I had to wash the dishes while I listen to her allegations.

Men go out and roam to moan under sheets and feel complete. See I'd rather cheat on you than beat on you because I'm not the violent type. I'd rather turn *her* over than turn over a new leaf and release unto you my massive frustration when it comes to you.

You are marveled by my patience, wondering why I continue to put up with your childish ways, yet while I am knee deep in another woman I, somehow, see brighter days.

That day never comes.

Orgasm wasted on "based it on my insecurities" type thought...and I am caught up...again.

The only friend of love is reason. The only friend of love is reason.

I need to learn that.

Eye to Eye

If I am a direct reflection of Christ then Christ must hurt a lot. He must flirt a lot with thoughts of hopelessness and cope with this best through poetic therapy. Cope with this the worst through trying to talk about it...Doubt it will be understood by mortal men so I write down my pain on papyrus. The virus in my pen is infecting my pad. I am glad to be blessed with the gift...yet I get sad when my literary riffs expose my fears. It usually brings me to tears. Eye to eye with my inner enemies...befriending me as if we walked to school together back in the days of innocence.

I wonder if God understands the demand I place on myself to be at least 3/5 of a perfect man, as my slave hands covers my, occasionally, blinded eyes. Blinded to the cries of my enemies, whom I was told to love in spite of. But is it possible?

I guess these are just the idiosyncrasies of a scorned man. As the mental meteor is sinking into the unforgiveness desert of my soul's torn land. Can I really pray without ceasing? Dreams of deceasing...Dreams of increasing Hell's population by one. By gun they kill my son with these crimes called "black on black"...and in my bank account I am lacking stacks, as blackened cats keep crossing my path...as the wrath of God seemingly awaits me. But God is love. Love is God. Love your enemies. Love your enemies. Love your enemies. Love your enemies. Love your enemies.

Your enemies hate you, but you love them. But do we hug then with arms that are subconsciously saturated with vengeful murder plots and what nots? God has got to deal with me.

Fallacies and abnormalities cause me to be a casualty of spiritual warfare...but momma always said that life wasn't fair. But does it get easier after a while?

Some laughter and a smile to cover up the hidden, guilt ridden, forbidden thoughts that make you lose focus. It's like hocus pocus voodoo hexes vex my soul, leaving the rest of the world on hold because I can't understand who I am. I am damned to Hades' holding cell...knowing well that my conscience is condemned. I am neglecting sex because I don't want to be a father to a fatherless seed.

I bother *this greed* that lies in other people...telling them that I cannot be everything to everybody. Dealing with these very naughty thoughts of giving the rest of the world a piece of my "yet to be redeemed" mind, as I evade time with lines of disgruntled poetry...procrastinating a fate yet to come.

I hum anthems and tribal chants as Bible lamps light up my bedroom at 5:27 in the a.m. It is similar to the September 11th mayhem that lies in my mind...and I am tired of crying.

I am tired of lying to myself telling my alias that everything is going to be okay when I know the day will come that I must face my demons...eye to eye.

Reality Check

I am hanging on by the withering thread of my confessions of "forever and ever", "through thick and thin"; "we will stick together no matter what". Yet I, with constant failure, try to weather my storms be it physical or emotional; but my visions of our future children living in poverty overshadows any fallacies of The Cosby Show scene.

My pipe dreams of an infinite bliss of family togetherness with you are messing up my natural sleep...as I wait to awaken from these nightmares of you trusting me with your life. "Wife" terrorizes me as I walk through valleys of the shadow of debt, as I set my affections on things above...all while dirty dancing at the bottom of the barrel acting as if I own the club. I am deceiving myself...while simultaneously digressing.

It is a blessing to have a companion of your virtuous caliber...you bring out the best in me...addressing me as the one and only king of your soul's empire.

Lately I have been indulging in an elusive dialogue with your female intuition; as she teases my manhood, relaying to my subconscious in spurts that soon my fears will be exposed.

The love we have made is so passionate and detailed, but in due time the voice in your thoughts of tomorrow will whisper to your spirit, "This is all he has to offer you."

I find myself dealing with you in the back of my mind in rapid succession. I try to sweet talk my way out of conversations about our future. You know...the ones you say are just a "normal" topic of conversation. They don't mean anything (or so you say). You are in no means rushing me, yet I am having flashbacks of the trip to the jewelry store and how you knew exactly what you wanted...one carat, platinum, etc. When those serious talks I elude you say I have an attitude. I just can't see that far; for my present condition are cirrus clouds in my window of tomorrow. I soak my sorrow through means of poetic verses to no avail.

I can't help but to love you. You are like this jewel in my life but I can't fit you into my soul's budget right now. It is not that your inner needs are beyond my ability of fulfilling. I know I must reap many dirty seeds that I have sown...thus I am making certain this is done without you as a co-recipient due to my immaturity.

I have secretly lusted after past girlfriends...ones that I know I can take full advantage of with no conscience. Yet, I find myself only wanting to share my life with you.

You have a grip on me; so tight that I can't move past these candlelit visions into the realm of "faith without works is dead". In essence...we are trying to live in this fictional world; while our non-fiction present is being overpowered by thoughts of what we may become.

You make it seem so fabulous, as I take a glimpse of our dreams. I see our two kids, each with their own room running around our immaculate home adorned with priceless African art, as their minds exceed far above that of their peers; reminding us of their grandparents with each glance into their eyes. Daddy's little girl and mommy's boy...

We are all wrestling in the den...Daddy and daughter versus mommy and son in a family tag team match. We grow tired from hours of playing...all while knowing *our* fun will but soon begin. The children are bathed and put to bed, as do we. We wash each other's body in the marble tub; making plans for our much needed vacation. You often talk of us making love by the moonlit window in the king size brass canopy bed while the babies are asleep. We are taking long trips to the ocean sands and blue streams in Jamaica...all while giving each other sweet kisses on the hotel room balcony. Sounds nice... and the visions alone make me mentally climax into realms of infinite glee. Yet again I begin to digress.

I am suffering from issues that cause me to throw in the towel. Contrary to our own popular belief; I see far beyond these dreams. Regressing at warp speed, I am afraid to take the next step. The baggage I carry is not only that of emotional ties with lost loves; it is also a questioning of my ability to spiritually head a home that has no foundation...only that of a man who can't see himself being authoritative. In my mirror I see failure...the denial of childhood fantasies that every boy wants makes me outwardly appear as if I am spoiled; but in essence I am searching that which was stripped as an adolescent. I have tried to compensate for these insecurities through my sexual prowess; only leaving me more inwardly scarred. I stand as a spiritual being whose sins and mistakes leave me fickle and consistently without purpose with dreams and ideas put on hold with a fearful procrastination as my accomplice.

I am lost. I am confused. I am the perfect candidate to warp your serene life.

It's not you... it's just...not me. I am a having a...

Reality Check

Time and I

3:12 in the a.m. can't sleep...deep thoughts. My mind's eyesight is in overdrive...Alive and well; healthy, yet no suggestion as to why I cannot travel into the nightly realm of *rapid eye movement.* Can't prove it; but I think something is wrong with me. Why long must it be? I don't know. Don't show me that picture again satan, I refuse to believe I have issues. I need tissues but I am not weeping...nor am I sleeping. Keeping focused on mangled visions. Decisions? Many. Incisions? Plenty...on my soul. I hold in my hand...nothing of value but this pen. Am I alone again? I am. I feel damned. I scram for a piece of paper and a pen because I feel like I am just a sin away from losing it all together. Falling forever in a mental Hades. These sentimental rabies is affecting my telepathy as I am communicating with diseased thoughts. Just me and my pen...and my friend that lies within who seemingly tortures my mental optimism...so I wonder am I my own enemy?

In me there lies poetic pain and literary lament and the scent of my pen's blood smells leukemic. Verse upon verse...uncontrollably multiplying line after line...rhyme after rhyme equals rhyme aftermaths...as the wrath that came from my pen makes no sense after the paragraph is read back. Dead smack in the middle of my heart is black pain. Is that rain drip-dropping? No. That is just the sound of my clock tick-tocking...letting me know that time never rests. Time never sleeps. Time never cheats. Time never beats out of synchronization. Time has never lied to me. Time will never lie to me. Time is never unfair. Time is always consistent with me. Time never goes behind my back and talks about me. Time keeps it real with me. That is what I like about time, time is always present...holding my hand and walking and talking to me.

Never would I compare myself to time but tonight time and I are soul mates. Time is all I have and I know that when everyone else is sleep...time will stay up with me. Time will sup and commune with me. Time will comfort and listen to the ailments of my soul. Time will read me bedtime stories. Time will kiss me goodnight. And when I wake up...time will be right next to me. However, time will be hung over. You see, last night...as a result of my poetic inebriation and taking shots of useless literary desperation, because of me...time got *wasted*.

Forgive me time.

To Find You

All I have to do is find you...then forever begins...

But I must find you first.

I already have half of our life mapped out with you bringing the other 50% because your input is as equally important as mine.

Better yet, I'll even go 49, because I am willing to give in for the sake of an argument.

I love you that much...

But I must find you first...

My rib count is off...

I must find you.

I put too much seasoning on the baked chicken.

I must find you.

My intuition pales in comparison to yours...

I must find you.

See I need you...

I don't want you...A "want" comes and goes.

A want is an upgrade from something I already have.

A want wavers...A want is picky.

A want wants too much...

A need sustains life...

I want a wife...but I need you.

I need you.

My dreams need your extra hour of sleep for more insight that I would have never seen.

During disagreements I willingly lose, so WE ultimately win in the end.

See, I want to be your friend. The one that asks if you need more cream in your coffee and laugh when you dance offbeat...

The one that will respond to your 3:37 am shoulder taps when you need conversation...

I must find you.

I must remind you that it will not work if any other man.

I was created to love you, serve you, and worship you.

I...am the only one that can calm you down.

I...am the only one knows exactly what to say to you without uttering a word.

You hear me through my eyes.

I don't care about you weight gain...You could care less if I weight train...Never been about the physical frame...Baby, you sustain me.

But...I must find you first.

I must bind your thirst for settling for the wrong man and have you drink of my soul's well that will never run dry.

And that's will starts in my eye.

Baby, I weep for you.

Those promises I will keep for you...

And over every bad relationship, over every heartbreak, and over broken promise...I will leap for you.

Just...catch me.

And then I will have found you.

I must find you.

You complete me.

To find you...

I must find you.

"Ode to Soul"

"I Just Called To Say I Love You"

I know you tired of me leaving you messages, expressing this love that I have for you, I'm getting plagued by the restlessness.

"Before I Let Go" let's follow this **Maze** down **Black Street**, take a right on **Beat(Street)**...sing a *"Song For You"* in *"Key of Life"*..."*In A Sentimental Mood*" but "*I Want To Rock With You*", getting drenched by the *"Purple Rain"*, *"Can You Stand* it*(The Rain)*?" Let's catch the *"Love Train."*

"Let's Stay Together", let me know *"What's Going On"* because *"I Feel For You"*..."*I Only Think Of You on 2 Occasions*"...day and night, that's **The Deal** with you.

We just *"Everyday People"* and *"Ordinary* (People)", *"My Cherie Amour"*, I'm *"Overjoyed"* it's you that I *"Adore"*...

"*Round Midnight*" let's watch "*When Doves Cry*", spray your name in "*Graffiti* (over this*) Bridge*" to the "*Mountain that ain't never High Enough*".

It's just "*Human Nature*" to "*Wanna Be Starting Something With You*" and when I'm "*Yearning For Your Love*" I feel "*Kind Of Blue*."

Because you're so "*Outstanding*",girl you knock me out...looks like another "*Love TKO*" so let's "*Turn The Lights Out*."

You "*Easy Like Sunday Morning*", Monday, Tuesday, Wednesday, Thursday, Friday, "*Saturday Love*" too "*Saving All My Love For You*." Just a "*Little Ghetto Boy*" with a "*Crush On You*", my love is unlimited, I hope I'm "*Never Too Much*" "*For You*. "Once, twice, "*Three Times A "Lady" Sings The Blues*" when I get "*Scandalous*" and become a "*Trouble Man*" you saw it coming cause you're a "*Natural Woman*".

The bachelor was running but I "*Stop*ped *In The Name Of Love*" because "*I Want You*" for more than "*Sexual Healing*" let's "*Save The Children*".

"One in a Million" ways to live, let's choose 'em all get *"Off The Wall" "When Love Calls"* and *"Wake Up Everybody"*.

Let's *"Rock Steady"* get **Ready For The World** because that's what *"We Are (The World)"* not too far is a *"Shining Star"* you're my **Earth, Wind** and *"Fire and Desire"*..."*Wanna Take You Higher*", than you've ever...been before, *"I Can't Let Go"*...I love you so...Open the door to this...musical Heaven. Feast on this lyrical leaven.

Step Away From The Mic

I gotta step away from this mic...recite from my soul and hold on for dear life.

Step away from this mic and let my voice project, my choice to neglect the poetic elements that are now relevant to my life.

Step away from this mic...I hear a young lady crying out for me...but I am scared to respond. She says sees me in her dreams rescuing me but I am...scared to respond.

She says, without a doubt, am eternally hers...but I am scared to respond.

She says happiness will be a hard element to accomplish without her but I am...scared to respond.

Scared to open up the scars that were implanted...Granted, I have tried but to no avail.

The veil has been placed over my eyes.

Step away from the mic...

The stage is my life...The mic be my solace.

I got to face it...Chase it and deal with it...like a man...Like a hand full of cards but ignorant of poker bluffs. I am cuffed to the table losing all of my soul's possessions...probably missing out on my blessings.

Stressing...

Digressing...

Depressing mood swings causes me to say rude things to people who love me regardless...

Thus

I

Must

Step

Away

From

This

Mic

I will yell if I have to so somebody can hear me...CLEARLY...sometimes I think only Jesus can.

Soaking in my own misery; seemingly visually impaired to the Light of Life...dealing with a heart full of sporadic strife towards "her." Lying to myself claiming that, "I am over that."

I scream, "forget it, forget her, forget them, forget him..."multiple times in my mind daily...but I can't help but to love.

Some have said I don't know what love is...possibly true.

But it has to be "you" to teach me...

But it has to be "you" to teach me...

But it has to be "you" to teach me...

Every "you" is different.

Impeach me. I can't control the holes in my soul's
nation...raging out of whack.

*tap   *tap   *tap

*tap   *tap   *tap

"Is this thing on?"

Step away from the mic.

I have to think about the drought that has consumed where
my spirit's river used to. Where the streams would flow
freely and I would bask in its splendor...a more gentler me.

Now I have grown cold...Grown old and bitter.

Chitter chatter, scattered throughout my mind sends me in
fits and just sits there idle.

Pressing down on my psyche like weights...causing me to go into crying fits...wanting to make a phone call to the one woman I KNOW will be there waiting.

He loves her...she is always in the audience waiting to hear him speak...but lately the stage lights have been dim. She is looking for him but he is hiding behind the curtain...hurting.

Scared to face the spotlight where his fears will be exposed.

Pop always told me that "life don't owe me nothing..." thus I am bluffing...trying to sweet-talk life for time to get it together.

There are two of me...The spoken and the broken.

Which

One

Do

You

Hear?

*tap   *tap   *tap

*tap   *tap   *tap

Is this thing on?

Inclined To Nurture

I have no problem stroking your female ego.

That is what I am supposed to do.

I worship you without blinking or reading the manual,
handing you poetic flowers and showers of what you have
never experienced from another man.

A gift...

To make you laugh...

To make you think...

To make you drink of my soul's well...

Inclined to nurture...

I have learned from seeing.

Human beings like to feel human.

Listening to you cry...

Knowing when not to talk...

Knowing when you are too weak to walk and I must carry
you...

Daring you to dream big...

Assisting with your future plans...

Blowing off the eraser debris when you edit your vision...

I listen.

Adoring you as if today has no expiration date...

And I will wait...until you...get it.

Inclined to nurture...

I will kiss you at odd times with no premise.

I will not cut you off ..."Go ahead and finish."

The lemons life has thrown us have been concocted into flavorful virgin daiquiris.

I get inebriated off of your theories.

See, I love your mind.

Inclined to nurture...

I will embrace your fears and wipe your tears and wait until you are sleep before I weep.

I must be the stronger vessel...while in your presence.

However...I will hide things from you.

I will slide things by you in conversation in a code only I can understand.

It's my way of admitting. My way of repenting...

My way of asking for forgiveness for re-nigging on promises...

Mother told me that some things should only be shared with God and the grave...Like when I didn't behave and brave acts of discipline were missing...and I fall.

Understand that I am the offspring of Adam, David, and Samson, and many others stories that didn't make the Biblical cut.... making me a mutt of many men...the butt of the joke from many sins.

I am not making excuses...I am simply making sense.

Considering the ratio of the thoughts I have versus the actions taken, I am doing very well.

I have restraint.

The pictures they sometimes paint, however, are elaborate and full of color and detail...challenging me for input.

Most times I decline.

However, sometimes I am inclined to intertwine my artistry and a part of me is splattered on strange canvas...leaving my soul's signature.

Understand that the God in me allows me to have a will and I still, at the most inopportune times, partake in Eden-like meals...then realizing I am unclothed.

Every man has his Eve.

Yet, it's never right to blame her.

Inclined to nurture...

Inclined to hurt her...without her knowing...

Suffering inwardly is me.

And I really do love you. I do.

Inclined to nurture.

Far Away

Why I am choosing to walk away from the greatest love I have yet to experience boggles me; for I know that You are what makes me whole. Knowing that the life I am now embarked upon consists of a dreadful and remorseful end, I can't comprehend the reasons why I still walk further and further away. Nostalgic about the things I used to cherish and strive for, I now find myself complacent in my wretched state. At times I feel like a reformed harlot; allowing myself to get re-infected with the issues I used to battle against, yet trying to come back to You. However, when I see the mistakes I have made, the past sins I once evicted now once again paying wages to my soul, I feel as if You are better off without me, for I feel as if I am a man incapable of truly committing to You.

I am far away.

I look back and remember the times when we were close, fellowshipping on a regular basis and spending quality time with each other, now our conversations are now a monologue, as I hear You calling me yet I answer not, for the shame silences me. I have been instructed the ways of getting back to the place where we can be one again, but it is a struggle for me, for climbing up is so much more a strenuous task than falling.

I am far away.

The words I feel You are speaking to me are saturated with clarity, yet I convince myself that the sins I now once again live cause me to be a blocked canal from Your voice. Where did I take that wrong turn that led me back to my evil ways? At what moment in time did I forget that You were reason for living? Why am I acting out the transgressions I used to testify about being free from?

I am far away.

Gazing into the mirror of my soul I see the inner stains of sin and filth taking their toll on my outer countenance, for my spirit is disfigured and my face displays it through dark shades of guilt only You and I can see. For only You know what happened, but because I feel like I am hearing impaired when You speak, I continue to walk spiritually blindfolded through shadows of death.

I am far away.

I know I need You to become once again free in my spirit...but because I have failed so many times before at a perfect relationship with You, I somehow feel better knowing that You didn't have to deal with my immaturity. I need Thee, but I don't want to continue to fail the tests. In essence, the course that was setout for me, I shall fail too.

In my confusion I often utter words that I don't understand. In my anger, I often say things I don't mean...yet out of the abundance of the heart, I speak. Was it that I was never really committed to You in the first place? I can't be so, for would I know I am far away if I had never experienced closeness to You? I need You, but I keep letting You down and I am raped in my subconscious daily for my folly.

I want to come back to Thee, yet the journey downward that started of slow took a long dive and has scarred my spirit immensely. For if I was to come back, would You even recognize me?

I am far away.

Restore me, my Father.

About Her Eyes

I wasn't sure whether to dap her up or hug her...smile or mean mug her. It's not that I mean mug only a regular basis...but the faces she was making to were quite intimidating.

But her eyes were so beautiful...

She couldn't hide that... Couldn't disguise that...Just like the sky is a fact...Just like the lies are stacked to distract what's fact...Like the fact that the "sigh" I extract from my soul is black because...her soul was out of whack; causing her to react like that.

And I wanted to tell her so badly...But I was madly jealous because she was neglecting her ovarian mechanics on overly popular inordinate tendencies probably backdated to being the innocent enemy of some wayward man.

Beautiful eyes...

Beautiful lies that were told and made her bold in her gender complications...Making mental compilations of why this is the best route for her to take...Make no mistake..."Born this way", so she say...And though she portrays a man... no substitute can dispute the truth that the proof lied within her womb.

And her eyes were so beautiful...

I am trying to telepathically reboot her mind by approaching her with, "Hey lady and hey baby..." type lines...Find ways to tell her she looks pretty; even though it's a pity that her soul's mainframe has been defamed and defragmented and my troubleshooting is having trouble shooting the polluting thoughts down to the ground zero of her soul that has made her so cold towards the brethren. So cold to the point where she barely responds if I approach her delicately...

I had to catch myself. I almost started looking at her as one of the boys.

The stems on my soul's tree were begging me to reach out and find the root of the issue. I would still see virtue while others would whisper and murmur behind her back. I would distract them with, "She still a woman" type dialogue. She still cycles once a month. She still get a smear once a year. She sheds tears when her feelings are hurt; thus I search self to not be a finger-pointer.

Someone's daughter has been deceived, hurt, scarred, marred in what they perceived to be love, drugged through the mug of emotional rainstorms. Pain forms and the norm is transformed to a deformed painting of hurt and the skirt is removed and the tattoo of rebellion is telling a story through real life skits...with terrible acting because she can't be what she was not created to be.

Her eyes were so beautiful.

The eyes never lie. The eyes never lie. The eyes of my soul have never told a fib, and she still has that extra rib that completes me....and what beats me is that what she may hate is what she so oddly tries to replicate.

And I want to tell her how beautiful she is to me but it's almost like I would be telling my homeboy because homegirl is in a world all her own.

And with all of the saggy pants...face minus the enhancement of cosmetics...The fiddy cap...The unlaced A1s, white tee to hide the "C" cups, and the occasional nose sniff and "head up"...One thing she can't hide is those eyes.

Her eyes were so beautiful...

So beautiful that I make a conscious effort to see her as the most beautiful woman that walks the face of that piece of Earth she treads at that very moment that I behold her. I think she needs me to hold her...but I'm scared to ask...so I'll just keep doing the task of...

Staring into...

Those...

Beautiful...

Eyes...

Eviction Notice

Here I am again...

This place...

This space where only me and my guilt fit...

Looking around wondering when the thundering is going to begin that will signal the end of my normal thought process...Got mess that needs to be dealt with...This gift and curse...

The hearse is parked within my psyche.

Waiting...

Don't know where to turn...the candle burns at both ends, which will singe my conscience...inevitably.

Nearing 30...still dirty it seems...I am.

Self-hurled vulgarities fill my mind and soul...wanting my spirit to take control and mold something great out of that which seems shapeless...

"Take this like a man..."something says... "You will pay"...I say...to self.

Death seems so fitting now...Sitting down...waiting...

Contemplating...debating...coordinating thoughts of meeting Him...with Him understanding...I had to.

"I had you"...I hear my mother whispering in my ear in my dreams...seems selfish to others but seems so picturesque to me...no longer dealing.

No longer feeling this pain, this torment. This war went from bad to worse, to worse, to worse, to hearse-filled visions of me peacefully resting in His bosom.

I'm too strong to be too weak minded to do it...

Through it all,

We fall down but we get up...The song is on mental repeat.

Infinitepeat...never-ending cycle...revival without the spirit...

Demons...know me on a first name basis.

I talk to God but rarely get that much needed dialogue...a monologue of shame I release to Him...grim reality...I have fallen beneath myself.

I need meditation...I want my revelation to be refilled...like my spirit...but...

I am depleted of both.

Why pray? Nothing seems to get answered...Cancered is my spirit...rotting at the core...more of the same blame game...The name on the guilty list? Mine.

Blind...

Need to see...

Need to be...cleansed thoroughly...

God I pray again...

Wash me.

Please.

I'm struggling down here.

You got me though, right?

Missed Destinies

They say that time is the interruption between 2 infinities...

Thus I cherish time...

Time...our richest commodity, but we always seem to build the camaraderie's with those who waste it...

Makes it difficult to pause....Time...

I spend much of my time doing rhymes...But the mime inside my spirit is speechless....reaches into my soul and screams but I don't hear it...

Missed destinies...

Riches and blessing seems to be the main topic of many folks...but they cannot quote their lost.....time.

Destinies are missed...The snake in our familiar garden hissed and we fell victim to their lair of deceit...

Defeat...missed destinies...

I sometimes wonder about whether or not I missed my destiny...or possibly God is testing me...Like He did Job...

Am I the servant that is being considered? After the grass withered I realized that it was not that green at all...Appalled at my mistakes I ask God for more....time.

Time...

But time is like a snowman that faces the sun on a July
noon...

Its goes away fast...

Missed destinies...

Blessed are we who learn to value time...

We are given second chances...

Like we are given second dances when the spiritual CD
skips and we dip at the wrong time...

Can I help you up?

Missed destinies...

There is no such thing as missed destiny if you realize it
while you are still breathing...

See...while we are impregnating our bad choices...our
destiny is still conceiving...it's self.

Not a missed destiny...a mixed trajectory...

God makes no mistakes.

The Happy Squirrel

A blind squirrel found a nut...and right beside the nut was a cream that could cure his blindness.

Being thankful for his meal; he realized that blindness wasn't that bad.

He then understood what happiness really meant.

www.ingramcontent.com/pod-product-compliance
Lightning Source LLC
Chambersburg PA
CBHW030921090426
42737CB00007B/272